CW00925942

PERMANENT SUPPRESSION OF FATNESS.

Please notice that word "permanent," stout reader; it is of vital significance.

Very likely you have found out the uselessness of trying to *cure* obesity—that is, achieve the *permanent* suppression of your fatness—by weakening dietary treatments; or perhaps you have tried in vain one of the many mineral drug remedies which are so dangerous and so futile, and have made yourself more or less seriously ill in consequence. These failures may have made you sceptical about any sort of obesity treatment.

Do not lose heart. You have not tried Antipon evidently. Thousands, however, have done so, and have had *lasting* reason to be thankful. Antipon, a pleasant liquid, quite harmless, is a unique combination of tonic and fat reducer; and, furthermore, it *outroots the obstinate tendency to abnormal fat development.*

After a course of Antipon one is not only reduced to normal weight and natural proportions; one is healthier and stronger, brighter and "fitter," while the clearness and pure hues of the complexion, the brightness of the eyes, the absence of all puffiness about the cheeks and chin and neck, show that the greatest beauty of all—the beauty of health—has returned for good.

The renewed slenderness of form, firmness and shapeliness of limb, grace of poise, and easy lightness of movement, denote the marvellous rejuvenating powers of Antipon.

The tonic effect of Antipon is exhibited in the improvement of appetite and digestion. One of the secrets of the success of Antipon is that perfect nutrition is re-established, and the subject eats more heartily both during and after the course of treatment, while the superfluous fatty matter is not less rapidly eliminated; nor will the excessive fat development recur when once Antipon has restored normal weight and proportions. There is a decrease from 8oz. upwards (according to degree of over-fatness) within a day and a night of taking the first dose of Antipon, which is purely vegetable and quite innocuous.

The famous scientist, Dr. Ricciardi, of Paris, writes:—" I must frankly say that Antipon is the only product I have ever met with for very quick, very efficacious, and absolutely harmless reduction of obesity. All other things are perfectly useless, and some absolutely dangerous."

Antipon is sold in bottles, price 2s. 6d. and 4s. 6d., by Chemists, Stores, etc.; or, in the event of difficulty, may be had (on remitting amount), privately packed, carriage paid in the United Kingdom, direct from the Antipon Company, Olmar Street, London, S.E.

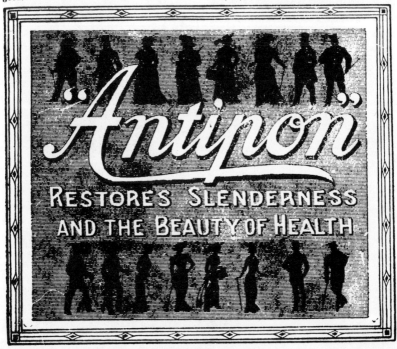

"Antipon" RESTORES SLENDERNESS AND THE BEAUTY OF HEALTH

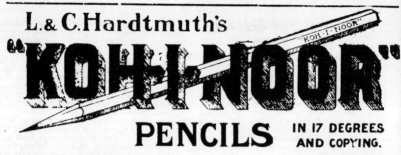

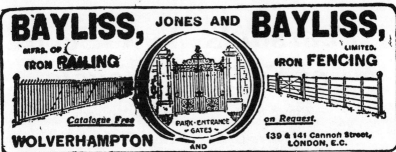

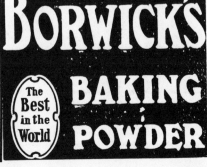

Stories
of the
Railway

Canon V. L. Whitechurch

(Photograph by courtesy of Mrs B. James)

Stories
of the
Railway

V. L. Whitechurch

Foreword by
Bryan Morgan

Routledge & Kegan Paul
London and Henley

Originally published in 1912 as
Thrilling Stories of the Railway

This edition
first published in 1977
by Routledge & Kegan Paul Ltd
39 Store Street,
London WC1E 7DD and
Broadway House,
Newtown Road,
Henley-on-Thames,
Oxon RG9 1EN

Printed in Great Britain by
Redwood Burn Limited
Trowbridge and Esher

ISBN 0 7100 8635 0

CONTENTS

		PAGE
I.	PETER CRANE'S CIGARS	11
II.	THE TRAGEDY ON THE LONDON AND MID-NORTHERN	29
III.	THE AFFAIR OF THE CORRIDOR EXPRESS	46
IV.	SIR GILBERT MURRELL'S PICTURE	63
V.	HOW THE BANK WAS SAVED	81
VI.	THE AFFAIR OF THE GERMAN DISPATCH-BOX	100
VII.	HOW THE BISHOP KEPT HIS APPOINTMENT	115
VIII.	THE ADVENTURE OF THE PILOT ENGINE	131
IX.	THE STOLEN NECKLACE	150
X.	THE MYSTERY OF THE BOAT EXPRESS	165
XI.	HOW THE EXPRESS WAS SAVED	180
XII.	A CASE OF SIGNALLING	191
XIII.	WINNING THE RACE	205
XIV.	THE STRIKERS	220
XV.	THE RUSE THAT SUCCEEDED	235

FOREWORD

The life of a country cleric at the beginning of the present century was a not unenviable one. Behind him lay the Darwinian controversy and the long struggle between the evangelical and tractarian wings of the Anglican church: invisibly far ahead was our present age of indifference and agnosticism. England was still a Christian nation and the pews were filled each Sunday. Not for nearly a century had a Laodicean peace so reigned in the church.

The stipend and perquisites of priest, parson, minister or whatever were, furthermore, usually adequate for his needs; and above all he had *leisure*. In 1800 he would probably have devoted this to blood sports; but in 1900 more humane standards prevailed and the clergy were more likely to engross themselves in studies of early church music or in chess problems. Yet for those with a certain talent the *cacodaemon scribendi* intruded to interrupt their prayers. To write on any subject – not for glory or even for money but because it seemed a natural activity which could be put aside when professional duties called – was hence a temptation to many turn-of-the-century clerics.

The whole subject deserves a monograph: was this widespread creativity connected, for example with the disappearance of the two-hour sermon? But certainly

few part-time authors could rival in quantity and
variety the *corpus* produced by Canon Victor Lorenzo
Whitechurch.

Whitechurch (and the 'Lorenzo' came from his half-
Spanish mother) was born on 12 March 1868, the son
of an East Anglian clergyman and the descendant of
men ranging from a painter of distinction to the Master
Gunner of England. He was educated at Chichester
Grammar School and then at the Theological College in
the same city, whence he was ordained deacon at the age
of twenty-three. Various curacies – mainly in the
Thames Valley – took this slim, very tall and dark-
haired man to 1904, when he attained his own cure of
souls at the attractive village and typically English
church of Blewbury near Didcot and his richest period
began.

Perhaps that cure was not over-demanding: but for a
man approaching forty, newly-promoted, not long
married and newly a father, his output was almost
prodigious. Already Whitechurch had published one full-
length detective novel, and in the nineteenth century he
had begun to produce short stories for markets ranging
from *The Strand* to the newly-founded *Railway Magazine*
and a humorous series for the *Boy's Own Paper*; but in
the decade after 1904, his production ran to a book a year
as well as many more short stories. The books, furthermore, covered a spectrum including crime, clerical lore,
the topography of those marvellous chalk downs, and
autobiography.

Was Whitechurch inspired to this diverse creativity,
one wonders, by the high and heady air of this corner of
the south-west – of Alfred's Wessex where 'seven sunken
Englands/Lie buried one by one' and where neolithic

trackways interlaced with the old Great Western single-track running down to Winchester? Had that flair for drama which made his liberal high Anglican sermons, delivered in resonant tones, a widespread attraction (and which also led him to produce and act in amateur Shakespeare and become a proficient amateur conjùrer) demanded a new outlet? Or had he suddenly acquired a gift of the Holy Ghost? Certainly he claimed to write 'without plan or premeditation', never quite knowing how his tales would turn out.

What is sure is that the short stories for which he is best remembered were written in this period for *Pearson's Magazine* and *Harmsworth's* and were published in 1912 as a collection under the title of *Thrilling Stories of the Railway*. (The British Museum catalogue, it should be noted here, drops the adjective, presumably as being an advertising gimmick rather than part of the title proper; and the present volume follows this usage except when forced to the 'thrilling' for facsimile purposes.) For these were the stories – mainly with a detective element – of an enthusiast for a subject which appeals to many schoolboys but which for the privileged few who are prepared to poke around yards and talk to signalmen becomes a lifelong interest.

The nexus between railways and the clergy (today including at least two bishops, and extended to include such fringe churchmen as organists) has been often remarked upon but never fully explained. Should one, for instance, accept the view of a current professor of scripture that the organisation of a railway is a microcosm of God's organisation of the universe, or agree with that vicar and author of popular children's books who claims that despite their faults the railways and the church are

the best ways of transporting a man to his final destination? Or should one look to the late Canon Roger Lloyd's
opinion that railway-lore is 'morally good in the sense
that it healthily occupies the mind and so becomes a
subsidiary and indirect cause of that self-forgetfulness
which is at the root of all virtue'?

Certainly, though, the clerical or lay enthusiast of the
early years of the present century was a happy man; for
Britain's railways were then at their peak of glory.
'Brief years, from the death of Queen Victoria to the out-
break of war', as Mr Hamilton Ellis has written, 'were
proud years. Enormous coal-trains rumbled and hand-
some expresses rushed about the country. Maintenance
was high and locomotives were often painted in gorgeous
colours.' *Bradshaw* ran to nearly 1200 pages (a figure
never preceded or exceeded) and in many a country
rectory stood as a work of reference beside *Crockford's*.
Numerous parsons stumped while drafting a sermon
must have relaxed intellectually by working out the
quickest route between Saxmundham and Blisworth.

But Whitechurch was no mere *Bradshaw*-browser: he
had become almost a practical railwayman. He knew how
to scotch a point, what was the loading-gauge of the
Great Northern and how long an engine took to re-water
as well as how to play model-trains with an eccentric
parishioner. And all this knowledge he transferred to his
pet detective, Thorpe Hazell.

Hazell is admittedly to a degree that cut-out figure, the
detective with a gimmick, whose prototype was the great
Holmes and whose like survive today. But he is made
more than two-dimensional by the number and variety
of his skills and oddities (which, it must be remembered,
have to be re-established every time in stories published
singly even if they become repetitive in a collected

volume). He anticipates Wimsey-*plus*-Bunter in his expertness with incunabula or camera, and adds the unique oddity of his health regime. For the most part his creator treats Hazell's Swedish drill and plasmon biscuits dryly and without overt comment: but in one exchange it appears that the Canon took a rather cynical view of what in the Shavian heyday was called a 'sanitary' or 'hygienic' life-style. Whitechurch is indeed often surprisingly relevant to the present day. Health cranks are always with us, and one suspects that Thorpe Hazell would have shown a more enthusiastic response than Victor Whitechurch to muesli breakfasts, fanatically anti-smoking doctors and the like.

But Hazell's primary characteristic, of course, is that which he shared with his creator – his knowledge and understanding of most aspects of railway lore (for Whitechurch was not really a locomotive man) from the apparent dryness of signalling procedure upwards. He is British fiction's only specialised railway detective, though he soon had an American rival: indeed, no less an authority than Ellery Queen has called him the first "speciality detective" of all. He does not, however, fill this book; for only about half of its contents, those of fairly pure detection, are "Thorpe Hazell" tales. The other half consists of stories where the accent is on adventure – and, interestingly, these often have a German villain since writers have always been more astute than soldiers and politicians in knowing where future menace lay. A few of these later tales could easily have been recast as Thorpe Hazell stories, but Whitechurch presumably wanted to divide intellectual from physical action. What binds the two classes is a shining, train-trodden ribbon of steel.

In 1913 Whitechurch left his beloved downlands to become chaplain to the Bishop of Oxford. He was to spend his life in that diocese. An honorary canonry of Christ Church followed, and he was on his way to becoming a minor prelate, hampered in cathedral duties only by his detestation of all forms of music. He then spent a comparatively quiet if busy war as a hospital chaplain, and at its close was promoted to the rural deanery of Aylesbury. Other honours followed; but still his pen would not be still, particularly during long morning sessions. And though the accent was now on full-length novels rather than short stories – and though too the Canon seems to have lost a little of his railway enthusiasm after the companies were forced to the defensive and he now preferred clerical settings for his mayhem – the book-a-year routine was observed as regularly and almost as ritually as a church festival right up to the author's death at the age of 65 on 25 May 1933.

In one respect Canon Victor Lorenzo Whitechurch has been atypical of the cleric whose prime fell about the time of the First World War: after his marriage to Florence Partridge, an artist who was to illustrate some of his books, he left instead of the usual quiverful only one daughter – Bertha, a distinguished artist in her own right who later married an eminent librarian and became Mrs James. But one need not be a Freudian to note how often those with superabundant creative energy are less philoprogenitive than the world's dullards. And there are better if harder ways of ensuring that one's name lives after one than flooding the world with sons.

For Whitechurch *does* have his immortality, and it is a greater one than that of Enoch Soames on his yellowing museum cards. As proof of this, he is mentioned in half a dozen definitive histories of detective fiction – American as well as British, for Whitechurch is probably even more prized in the US than here as a pioneer of immaculate plotting and factual accuracy: he was one of the first writers, for example, to submit his manuscripts to Scotland Yard for vetting as to police procedure. Of distinguished individual admirers there can be added to the name of Ellery Queen those of Dorothy L. Sayers, John Carter and others; and their enconomia have centred particularly on Whitechurch's railway stories. Yet for many decades the contemporary editions of *Stories of the Railway* have been becoming increasingly rare, and for the last fifteen years or so have become so much a bibliophile's rarity that anyone who finds a copy in his attic or in a country bookseller's shop has found treasure. Carter, for example, called the book "remarkable and inexplicably neglected", and over thirty years ago Scribner's catalogue described it as "rare and important".

Such, then, is the case for the present reprint. With the exception that a few small adjustments have been made in the preliminary pages of the book in order to accommodate these prefatory notes, it is a facsimile copy and not a reset version of the original. This course – in any case enforced economically – has perhaps both advantages and disadvantages: type-styles and conventions of punctuation (for example, the setting of "exercises" in quotes) change and call for a little nostalgic adjustment by the reader, but as against that he is assured that he is getting, untouched by human hand, a copy precise even to page-size of a work which he would be most fortunate otherwise to possess.

In conclusion, Whitechurch – that amiable and (as one story set in a strike shows) supremely fair-minded yet

slightly exotic man – would have been the last to claim
that he was a great writer. But he was a very good one,
and perhaps more important historically than he realised.
It is a personal pleasure to *not* rescue from oblivion, but
make available this fragment which represents perhaps
one thirtieth of his total output; and I believe that this
pleasure will be shared by three readerships in particular.

First there are the railway enthusiasts, that large band
who revel in the *minutiae* of Britian's railways (even
when the Canon chose to disguise their names) in their
years of glory. Second are the specialists in detective
fiction and particularly in the activities of the 'rivals of
Sherlock Holmes' – another substantial group. And
finally there are the clergy; for I would be surprised if
many copies of this reprint did not find their way to
vicarages, presbyteries and other priests'-holes.

I sincerely hope that I am right in this prediction.
For there will be no harm in a little professional support
for my own prayers that the soul of Victor Lorenzo
Whitechurch, a man born well over a century ago and
dead now for more than forty years, may – like so many
of the lines he loved – repose in peace.

Inadequate as this note has been, it would not have been
possible without much willing help from others. As so
often, for example, I am most deeply indebted to Mr
Brian Doyle for his encyclopaedic knowledge of crimino-
logical literature and to Mr Timothy O'Sullivan for his
invaluable services as liaison officer between myself and
the publishers. I have only had to ask my step-daughter
Kate Morgan to check one fact to set her off on a day's
diligent hunting : it was through her, for instance, that
we enlisted the aid of Mr C. H. Watson, obituarist to
The Times and himself a Whitechurch enthusiast. The

librarian of Christ Church, Oxford, and the editor of *Crockford's* have also put themselves out to help me, and the first edition from which the present facsimile is printed was kindly made available by the Bodleian Library. But my greatest debt of all is to Mrs James, who has with unfailing courtesy and accuracy replied to all those seemingly-impertinent questions to which answers must be found if a man is to be more than an entry in reference books.

B.M. 1976

Stories of the Railway

I

PETER CRANE'S CIGARS

A SLIGHT, delicate-looking man, with pale face and refined features, light red hair, and dreamy blue eyes.

Such is a brief description of Thorpe Hazell, book-collector and railway enthusiast, a gentleman of independent means, whose knowledge of book editions and bindings was only equalled by his grasp of railway details.

At least two railway companies habitually sought his expert advice in the bewildering task of altering their time tables, while from time to time he was consulted in cases where his special railway knowledge proved of immense service, and his private note-book of such "cases" would have provided much interesting copy to publishers.

He had one other peculiarity. He was a strong faddist on food and "physical culture." He carried vegetarianism to an extreme, and was continually practising various "exercises" of the strangest description, much to the bewilderment of those who were not personally acquainted with his eccentricities.

With this brief introduction of the man, it is proposed to set forth, for the first time, a selection of railway "cases" in which he played a more or less prominent part.

*   *   *   *   *   *

"I tell you I only paid fivepence each for them."

Harry Brett took the cigar from his customer's hand, looked critically at it, smelt it, and then shook his head decidedly.

"Can't be done!" he said, "must be a fake."

"Unroll it—you're welcome."

The young tobacconist broke the cigar in half, rubbed the leaves between his palms, and examined them carefully.

"Ye—es," he admitted, "it's right enough. Same leaf all through."

"What did I tell you?"

Harry Brett turned round, reached for a box on a shelf, took it down, and selected a cigar, which he compared with the fragments lying on his counter.

"Same brand," he said at length. "But I can't make it out at all. Now, I can't afford to sell these under sixpence each, or sevenpence from a broken box, and even then the profit's a mere nothing. You must have got these over the water Mr. Wilson?"

"No, I didn't."

"You couldn't have bought 'em retail at the price."

"I did, though."

"What, at a shop?"

"Yes."

"Where?"

"In this town."

"In Netherton?"

" Exactly."

" By George ! Who was it, Mr. Wilson ? "

" Well, at Crane's, if you want to know. There's no secret about it."

Harry Brett brought down his fist on the counter with a bang that made the scales rattle. The mention of Crane's name had evidently upset him.

" It's all very well," he said, " but I tell you it can't be done. Either Crane's a bigger fool than I took him for, or he means having you in the end, and is only running this sort of thing to advertise his business. Why, he hardly knows anything about the trade ; he's only been in it six months. You're welcome to buy them, Mr. Wilson, of course. *I* can't do them at the price."

" Well," returned the customer, " I'm a bit of a judge of a weed, and if he begins palming off inferior stuff he won't impose on me. But till then I'll save my money and deal with him. But, as he makes no reduction in other goods, I'll take a tin of my usual mixture from you."

" Oh, go and get your baccy where you buy your cigars," exclaimed Harry Brett, who had been working himself up into quite a rage. " I don't hold with all this underselling business, nor with those who encourage it. Good morning, sir ! "

Mr. Wilson smiled slightly at the young man's outburst of passion, shrugged his shoulders, and walked out of the shop.

Harry Brett leant on the counter with his elbows, gazing angrily at the fragments of the object which had upset him so much. He had been a tobacconist from his boyhood upwards, having begun to work in his father's shop ever since leaving school, and since his father's death, three years previously, he had come into the business. It was not a very large one, but it was well established, and had many old customers. And Harry himself had been calculating for some little time that there was profit enough out of the shop to support two, besides which he had a very distinct notion of the choice of a partner.

But for the last three months certain things had troubled him. His takings had grown distinctly less, and certain customers had become irregular. And it was a curious coincidence that these troubles had begun to date from the time when Peter Crane had opened a rival business in Netherton, with an announcement that during the first week he would give away a "tip-top cigar" with every quarter of a pound of tobacco purchased.

It was galling, inasmuch as this Peter Crane had nothing to recommend him. Netherton knew him as a ne'er-do-well, turning up every now and again at his widowed mother's, who kept a small confectionery shop in the town. He had cleared one window of this shop of its contents, and substituted the fragrant weed in its various forms, and, as often as not, his mother dispensed these goods, for there were intervals during which Peter Crane himself seemed to abandon his new trade.

"Well, Brett," said a quiet voice, suddenly, "you seem wrapped in thought. What is puzzling you? Half a minute, please, before you answer. It is time for my mid-day exercise."

Brett looked up at Thorpe Hazell, who had entered without noise, and now stood before him twirling his arms rapidly round his head and then suddenly thrusting them out in front. Hazell lived at Netherton, but had a little bachelor flat in town, where he spent a good deal of his time. He was a regular customer of Brett, who knew his little eccentricity.

When he had finished Brett told him about the cigar and his suspicions. Hazell leant on the counter and listened attentively.

" I know this young Crane," he remarked, " and I'm afraid he doesn't bear the best of characters. Of course, this affects your trade?"

" It does, sir, to a certain extent."

" Do you suspect anything?"

" Well, sir, I hardly like to say. This particular brand of cigar can be picked up very cheaply in Holland or Belgium, and if they could be got over without the duty I could understand it."

" You think it's a question for the Revenue officials?"

" Oh, *I'm* not going to put them on his track," said Brett scornfully. " There's honour in trade as in other things. Besides which, if there were nothing in it I should pose as a spiteful sort of chap, and it would be all the worse for me."

" I see. You've excited my curiosity, Brett. Well, I want some cigarettes of the usual brand— thank you. If you hear anything about Crane's movements you might let me know. And, by the way, don't talk about the thing. Good morning."

On his way home he called in at Crane's shop. Here he made a trifling purchase. Mrs. Crane served him.

" H'm," he muttered to himself as he regained the street. " That collarette of hers was genuine Brussels lace. I wonder whether Brett's suspicions are correct. It may be a case worth investigating."

Netherton was about twenty-five miles from

London, on the Mid-Southern and Eastern Railway, and Thorpe Hazell constantly ran up to town. On this particular evening he was due at a meeting at Kensington.

He had scarcely taken his seat in the train when a young man came in and sat opposite. Hazell glanced at him over his paper, and recognised him as Peter Crane. He remembered Brett's little difficulty for a moment, but dismissed the subject as he resumed his paper.

Now, when the train drew up at the London terminus of the Mid-Southern and Eastern Railway, Hazell did not hurry himself in the least. He was not due at Kensington just yet, so he determined to wait till the departure of the Continental train. There were many things to interest him. The type of engine running, the number of coaches—dozens of details that are only apparent to the enthusiast or railway matters.

He was standing on the platform, taking in these various things, when he suddenly caught sight of Crane going into the Continental booking-office. An impulse seized him, and a moment or two later he was standing close behind the tobacconist, over-hearing him ask for a return ticket to Gantes. He began to be interested.

" Now," he reasoned to himself as he went out of the station and took a hansom, "there's evidently a bit of clever smuggling going on here. Let's think. A return ticket. *How* does he get the cigars through? How does he bring them back? Seems to me there's a chance of a railway mystery here. Of course, it may be on the boat, but I shouldn't think so. I'll have a look into this. There's any amount of frontier smuggling on Continental railways, I know. I once saw half a hundredweight of tobacco fixed under a passenger coach on the St. Gothard, and beautifully run through Chiasso. This may be well worth investigating."

Once having made up his mind, Hazell lost no time in making further inquiries as soon as he returned to Netherton, the result being that he ascertained that Crane had a regular date in the month for absenting himself from home.

And so it happened that the next time the latter took a return ticket to Gantes, Thorpe Hazell, disguised in a black wig, and looking very much like a commercial traveller, was already seated in the Continental train, booked through to the same destination. He had his eyes wide open, and had already taken in the fact that Crane's luggage consisted of a fair-sized brown Gladstone, and a very large black kit bag.

Hazell kept well out of Crane's way all the journey, for he knew very well that it was the return trip only that demanded careful scrutiny. So he snatched what sleep he could. They reached Gantes in the small hours of the morning, and Hazell noticed that Crane put the kit bag in the cloak-room, after which he proceeded to an adjacent hotel, a porter carrying his Gladstone.

Hazell, whose luggage was quite small, looked about him, noticed a hotel just opposite, rang up the sleepy night-porter, and took a front room, so that he could command the entrance of Crane's hotel. Instead of undressing, he opened his bag, changed into a tourist's knickerbocker suit, and then lay down on his bed with a determination not to sleep more than a couple of hours.

At daybreak he was at his window, keeping

careful watch. An hour or two passed, and then his patience was rewarded. Crane came out of the hotel, smoking a cigar and suspecting nothing.

The next minute Hazell was in the street, following his prey to the station. He lounged into the booking-office in time to hear Crane take a return ticket to Antburg.

Then he inquired of the booking-clerk casually whether one could take a return to Antburg and come back the next day.

"No, monsieur, tickets are only available for one day."

He shrugged his shoulders lazily, for he never believed in taking too much trouble over anything. It was clear that Crane would be back in Gantes that day. The only thing was to find out whether he took his black bag with him. He did.

"Now," said Hazell to himself, as he went back to his hotel, "that young man is precious shrewd. It's pretty clear he's gone over to Antburg to get his goods—there isn't a better place in Northern Europe for getting them—probable out of bond, too. But why does he take this route? It's a roundabout way to get to Antburg. I know. He works the trick on the Mid-Southern and Eastern, and the other line won't do. It's well worth finding out, but I can't do anything yet."

He had his breakfast, strolled round the town, and finally came back to his room. He had jotted down the times of trains returning from Antburg.

Then he settled himself to perform a "nerve-strengthening" exercise, which consisted of lying down on the flat of his back and holding a tumbler of water, filled to the brim, over his head for ten minutes at a time, the object being not to spill a drop of it. He entirely abstracted himself from the object in hand, except at such times as Antburg trains were due, when he got up and carefully watched the street leading from the station.

In the afternoon Crane appeared once more and entered his hotel. Then Hazell paid his bill, went to the station, and waited for the train back to England. He was keen and alert now. If that black bag, which he surmised was in the cloak-room, contained cigars, he was particularly anxious to see how the Customs were evaded.

Exactly in accordance with his surmises, Peter Crane came down to the station in time for the afternoon boat train.

And this is what he did. He took the black bag out of the cloak room and *registered it through to London*. That meant that until the bag reached London he could not possibly get at it, and then he would have to open it in the presence of the Customs' officials, through registered luggage being examined there, and not at Dovehaven. The brown bag, which appeared to be heavy, he took in the train with him.

Thorpe Hazell began to be mystified. Assuming the bag to be filled with cigars, he could see no way in which they could be brought through free of duty. He watched the luggage being taken on the boat at Ozende, but Crane was absolutely regardless, and had thrown himself on a saloon berth, and was sleeping almost immediately, his brown bag beside him.

At Dovehaven the examination of hand luggage took place, and Hazell had squeezed himself close beside Crane in order that he might see what was in the brown bag. There was nothing suspicious. It contained quite a pile of books and articles of clothing, a pink shirt being rather conspicuous.

As soon as the examination was over Crane turned to the porter who was carrying the bag.

" Put that in the van," he said. " Label it for London. I shan't want it in the carriage with me."

Hazell, still wondering, now went up to the guard's van and watched the luggage being put in, both of Crane's bags being among them. The guard himself was busily engaged helping the porters, as the boat was rather late, and he was anxious to get off.

" Now then, sir, are you going on ? Take your seat, please. Right away ! "

A shrill whistle, a wave of the green lamp, and the train was off, the next stop being the London terminus.

" Curious," said Hazell to himself as he took a packet of plasmon chocolate, and a flask of milk out of his bag a d proceeded to "dine." " Perhaps I'm wrong, after all. Ah ! "—as a thought struck him—" well, we'll wait till we get to town."

A couple of hours later that night the train drew up at the London terminus, having, of course, run through Netherton without a stop. Behind the long barrier stood a number of Custom House officials waiting to examine the registered luggage before it was passed through. Hazell watched by the guard's van until Crane's two bags were deposited on the platform. Crane took charge of the brown one himself, and a porter followed him with the black one to the examination counter. Hazell stood a little behind, eagerly awaiting the result.

"Anything to declare, sir ? Tobacco, scent, cigars ? "

"No—nothing."

"Open your bag, please."

"Certainly."

He unlocked the large black bag and threw it open. Hazell bent forward. And he caught a glimpse of a pink shirt—and books.

The black bag contained the identical articles that he had seen in the brown bag at Dovehaven.

A solution struck him. Glancing round he saw a platform inspector whom he knew. Rushing up to him he exclaimed, in a whisper :

"Jarvis—I'm Mr. Hazell—look here."

"Lor', sir, I shouldn't have known you. I——"

"Hush. Don't let on, man. Quick; you see that fellow in the light overcoat doing up his bag. Get one of those officers to examine the brown bag by his side. Sharp!"

The next moment Jarvis was behind the counter and had spoken a word to the official. Crane had just strapped up his bag and was moving off. Hazell had darted away.

"Sir—one moment."

"What is it ? "

"That other bag. I want to see it."

"It's not registered luggage. It was examined at Dovehaven. Here's the chalk mark on it."

"Never mind. Open it, please."

"Oh! very well," cried Crane with a laugh, laying it down on the counter and unstrapping it. "Here you are."

The official looked inside, his face burst into a smile.

"All right, sir!" he exclaimed, "that's soon settled."

Jarvis, who was standing by, smiled too. A minute later Hazell accosted him.

"Well," he asked, "what was inside that bag?"

"Nothing, sir. It was *empty!*"

"Empty was it? Oh! please say nothing about this, Jarvis."

He went into the refreshment-room, ordered a cup of coffee, lit a cigarette, and sat down to think it over. For once in his life he was completely baffled. It had seemed quite simple to him as he came up in the train, and he had thought that the opening of the brown portmanteau would prove the solution of the enigma. After a while a plan of action developed in his mind, and he went out of the refreshment-room. Jarvis was still on the platform.

"Jarvis," he said, "I don't want it known that I came up by the boat train to-night."

"Very well, sir."

Jarvis knew of more than one railway mystery in which Thorpe Hazell had been involved, and was to be trusted.

"Thought you'd caught a bit of smuggling, sir?" he asked.

"Oh!" drawled Hazell, "I was a little suspicious, that was all. Capital run up to-night."

"Yes, sir. Bob Nobes is a good driver."

"Ah! The guard was smart with the luggage at Dovehaven."

"John Crane, sir? Yes. He's one of our best guards. Runs this train in regular shifts."

Hazell's eyes sparkled for a moment.

"You—er—didn't see what became of that young man?"

"Yes, sir. Got into the train on No. 2 platform."

"Ah, that's mine, I believe, to Netherton. Good-night, Jarvis."

He got into the train, a smile of satisfaction on his face. He meant to master this little mystery.

  *   *   *   *   *   *

A couple of days later he was buying cigarettes.

"Oh, by-the-way, Brett," he said, "I think I can promise you that your hated rival will shortly shut up shop."

"Indeed, sir! Well, I shouldn't be sorry. I've lost half my trade in cigars."

"Ah! Oh, I say, Brett, there's a fellow named John Crane—something on the line. Know him?"

"Peter's cousin, sir."

"I see. Well, keep your mouth shut, and let me know when Crane goes away from home. I think we might have quite a little bit of fun then."

Three or four weeks later Thorpe Hazell received a note from Brett. In answer to it he wrote:

"Come round to my house to-morrow at about 8 p.m. Bring a great coat."

The tobacconist duly turned up, and found Hazell in his study.

"Sit down, Brett. Have some toast and water. No? Well, then, take one of your own cigarettes."

"Thank you, sir."

"I ordered the dog-cart for 8.30," went on Hazell. "We have quite a drive before us. That's why I mentioned your great coat."

"What are we going to do, sir?"

"You'll see all in good time."

They were soon bowling along the high road in the opposite direction from that of London. Hazell had the reins, and was not disposed to be communicative. After they had gone about seven or eight miles, Hazell turned down a by-road.

"You know where this leads, Brett?"

" Across Pinkney's Common, sir."

" Exactly."

Presently he said :

" There are the lights of the main line signals ? '

" Yes, sir."

A couple of red lights stood out in the blackness of the sky.

" And there's the level crossing ? "

" Yes, sir."

" All right. We'll put o⁻   ₁ps out."

He drew up to perform the operation.

" Good, and now we're going to drive on the grass across the common. And don't speak above a whisper, please."

They drew nearer the line. On their left, where the road crossed the railway, the bright light of the gatekeeper's-box was discernible. Presently Hazell pulled up.

" We'll tie the cob to this tree," he whispered. " That's right. We shan't have long to wait."

" It's a lonely place," said Brett.

" Quite so. We don't want to go close up to the line. This will do. It's the up-train we want."

Wondering what was going to happen, Brett waited.

Presently Hazell said : " Here she comes. Those are her headlights. Now you watch what happens. Keep your eyes open."

A white light above a green appeared in the distance, and grew brighter every moment. Then there was a roar as the approaching express bore down upon them. The train was running on a slight embankment, and they could see along its whole length.

" Look ! " said Brett suddenly, " one of the doors is open—in the last carriage."

"Exactly. The guard's van, Brett. There he stands. Look out! Ah! There's a pretty little smuggling dodge for you."

As the train swept by they could distinctly see the guard silhouetted against the light in his van. He appeared to be leaning out of his door, holding some large and heavy object. The next moment he had dropped this on to the soft turf of the embankment. As the train rushed by the crossing, a green light appeared for a moment, held out of the guard's van, and turned towards the rear of the train.

"Now," exclaimed Hazell, "we'll just wait and see what happens. First of all, we'll get as close as we can to that package—ah!—here it is. A convenient bush to hide us, too. He's coming, Brett!"

A man, carrying a lantern, came with a limping gait from the box at the level-crossing. Every now and then he paused, as if looking for something. Presently he gave a grunt of satisfaction as the light fell on a package lying on the grass.

He was just about to pick it up when Hazell stepped forward and said, very quietly:

"How much do you get for your share in this little transaction, my man?"

"Good Lord!" exclaimed the other, dropping his lantern in his fright. Hazell picked it up and turned it on him.

"Ah, you've a wooden leg, I see. No use to try to run. I suppose you were to keep this little lot till Crane came for them?"

"Don't—don't be hard on me, sir. I don't know nothin' about the contents—I—I—if you split to the company, sir, I'd lose my post."

Hazell laughed.

"Answer my first question, man. How much do you get out of this?"

"Ten bob a time," faltered the delinquent.

"Poor pay for the risk! How long has Crane been running this?"

"Six or seven months, sir."

"I see. Well, I'm afraid he won't find this little lot to-morrow. You can tell him when he comes for them that we've forestalled him. I should advise you to get your half-sovereign out of him before you tell him. And you can also add that if he wants to get them again he'd better call at Somerset House. Good-night—here's your lantern."

"I shall lose my post, sir."

"Not this time. You may think yourself lucky, though. Here, Brett, give me a hand with this parcel."

They carried the bundle, which was securely corded in thick American cloth, to the trap, and drove home. An hour or so later they were sitting in Hazell's study.

"I think we're entitled to one each before I send them to the Customs," said Hazell, selecting a cigar. "Now, how much do you think he cleared out of this lot?"

Brett looked at the four dozen boxes.

"Well, sir, if he got them, as you say, at Antburg, I can pretty well guess the price he paid. He ought to have saved quite twenty-five pounds in duty—very likely more. Altogether, the run was worth at least fifty pounds. But how did you find it out, sir?"

Hazell told him of his journey to Gantes and of the Customs examination in London.

"I own I was baffled for the moment," he said, "but, of course, I knew that he wouldn't have taken that journey to bring back an empty bag. Inquiry confirmed my suspicions that the guard was in it, possessing a duplicate key to the black bag, and I saw where the solution was. Undoubtedly the cigars were in the country, the only question was their whereabouts.

"The problem was very simple. I had only to keep a watch on Crane. He didn't notice the cyclist who followed him when he took a trap from here the next day, nor did he see that same cyclist lying behind a bush on Pinkney's Common with a field-glass watching him get a parcel from the level-crossing box. The rest you know. I guessed pretty accurately where the guard dropped them, and here they are."

"There's one thing I don't understand, sir," replied Brett, "and that is, why the guard didn't put the cigars in the brown bag and throw that out —or, in fact, why he took two bags at all."

"Oh, but that was where his greatest artfulness came in—the subtlety of the whole thing. The black bag was weighed at Gantes, and its weight registered. It was necessary to have a corresponding weight to it when it arrived in London. That's why he carried those heavy books and used the other bag for them.

"Then he and the guard knew perfectly well that detectives are pretty sharp in these matters, and if it had been noticed that he started back with two bags and only one arrived, especially as he was doing this more than once, suspicion would have been aroused. That's why the other bag was not thrown out. The whole thing was beautifully planned. Now we'll pack up—stop, though—I want three or four more of those cigars. That's right."

He packed up the cigars, and directed them to H.M. Customs.

" There," he said, " we'll send it anonymously. I expect, after his little visit to Pinkney's Common crossing, Master Crane will take a holiday. I must really thank you, Brett, for having given me an interesting little problem. I don't think we need take any further action. The three of them will have quite fright enough to stop them. Good night ! "

Hazell was right. Peter Crane suddenly disappeared from view, and the tobacco window was devoted to confectionery again. Harry Brett's prospects so increased with the return of custom that he made a formal proposal for the partnership, which was duly accepted, and the deed signed in the vestry of the parish church. Some weeks after the incident Thorpe Hazell was on the platform of the London terminus of the Mid-Southern and Eastern Railway, watching the incoming of the Continental express. As soon as the bustle was over, he strolled up to the rear guard, who was standing by his van.

" Have a cigar, guard ! " he said, offering his case.

" Thank you, sir."

" Take three or four. They're more yours than mine."

" What, sir ? "

" I believe you dropped them out of your van —some weeks ago—just by Pinkney's Common crossing. Good-night ! "

He turned his head when he reached the end of the platform. There was Guard Crane, standing like a statue, gazing at him with a paler face than was caused by the electric light.

II

THE TRAGEDY ON THE LONDON AND MID-NORTHERN

THORPE HAZELL opened his paper lazily as he breakfasted on boiled rice and wholemeal bread in his little West-end flat one very cold winter's morning in January. His interest in passing events was not very much excited until in turning a page he found himself confronted with the headlines:

SHOCKING ACCIDENT ON THE RAILWAY

SAD FATALITY

Folding the paper and shifting his seat so that the electric light fell better upon it, for it was rather dark, and his breakfast was an early one, he read as follows:

" A terrible occurrence took place on the London and Mid-Northern Railway last evening. As the express from London, due at Manningford at about a quarter past eight, was entering the station, those on the platform noticed a man leaning out of one of the windows, apparently in the act of opening the door of his compartment, and more than one porter shouted a warning to him to wait until the train stopped.

" When, however, the carriage had come to a standstill, he remained motionless, and those

who were near noticed, to their horror, that the
well-known white panels adopted by this company
were stained with an ominous colour, while blood
was trickling from the man's head.

"Assistance was rendered at once, but it was
soon seen that the unfortunate passenger was quite
beyond the reach of recovery, although it was the
opinion of a doctor who happened to be on the
platform that life could only have been extinct for a
few minutes.

"The victim of this terrible tragedy was, as has
been described, leaning out of the window, his arms
and head hanging over the door, which had to be
unlocked before he could be taken out.   There was
a bad wound in the back of his head and neck, as
though he had received a violent blow, and a piece
of one of his ears had been torn off.

"He had been travelling alone in a first-class
compartment, and held the return half of a ticket to
Manningford. All Manningford tickets are collected
at Bridgeworth, about ten miles up the line, the
last stopping station before Manningford, and
inquiries have shown that the inspector on duty
there had duly taken his ticket, so that he must have
met with his death during the last ten miles of the
journey.

"The guard of the train states that, on his own
request, he locked the compartment at the London
terminus just before the train started, and declares
that the unfortunate passenger was quite alone
during the whole of the journey.   His identity has
not yet been proved, but, apparently, he is a
foreigner. He is tall and dark, with a military-
looking moustache, is about fifty years of age, and
has a slight scar on his right cheek.

" He had no luggage, and the few papers found upon him were, we hear, written in French, but give no clue to his identification. These papers are in the hands of the police, and the body has been removed to one of the company's offices pending the inquest.

" As to the cause of death, the authorities are inclined to the belief that it was an accident caused by his own carelessness, but nothing definite is yet known. Between Bridgeworth and Manningford there are several bridges over the line, and it is conjectured that his head must have come into collision with the brickwork of one of these structures while looking out of the window.

" It will be remembered that a similar fatality took place near Liverpool some years ago, resulting in the death of a prominent citizen.

" On some of the Continental lines the windows are wisely barred, and in view of the liability to such unfortunate accidents, the railway companies would do well to adopt some means for the prevention of passengers leaning out of windows.

" The inquest will probably be held to-morrow."

Hazell laid down the paper, and sipped his lemonade thoughtfully. It was one of his fads always to take lemonade with his breakfast. Then he read the article through again, and pondered yet more.

" Struck his head against a bridge, eh ? " he said to himself. " That's very curious. Wound on back of head and ear torn off. Umph, I'd like to know a little more about this. Let's have a look at Bradshaw—ah ! I can catch that easily. It is not very far down to Manningford, and I know something of Rolfe, the divisional superintendent.

It's worth the journey—and there's plenty of time for ten minutes' dumb-bell exercise first."

Half an hour later he was in an express running down to Manningford. As soon as he had passed Bridgeworth he opened the window and kept a careful look out.

" Let's see," he said, " ah, of course, it would be the left side of the train—here's the first bridge "—and he put his head out and looked back—" plenty of space there. Well, we shall see presently."

Altogether he counted four bridges between Bridgeworth and Manningford. Arrived at the latter station, he made his way to the office of the divisional superintendent and sent in his card. Five minutes later he was talking with Rolfe.

" Ah," said the latter, " I expect I can easily guess what brings *you* down here, Mr. Hazell. But I assure you it's not worth the trouble of a journey. The thing's as plain as daylight."

" Oh, you think so, do you ? " replied Hazell.

" Why, we've found out everything. There's no doubt that the poor fellow put his head out of the window, and that the bridge caught it as he ran through."

" Which bridge ? "

" The second one from here."

" Indeed. And what makes you so certain about it ? "

" Why, we've found all the necessary traces."

" And what were they ? "

" Several bloodstains on the ballast of the permanent way and sleepers. Just where one would have expected them to be ; that is to say, about ten to twenty yards this side of the bridge. The train was running about fifty miles an hour, and the blood wouldn't drop at the actual striking-place."

" Was there any trace on the bridge itself ? "

"Not a bit. But that's not at all necessary. Just the corner would have struck him, you see."

" How about the missing piece of his ear ? "

" That's been found, too. I tell you there is no mystery about it. It's not in your line at all, Mr. Hazell."

" Ah, well—have you found the reason why he put his head so far out of the window ? For he must have stretched it out pretty well to strike it against the bridge."

" Oh, really, Mr. Hazell, that's a mere detail. There are hundreds of reasons why silly persons put their heads out of a train window. You see it done every day."

" I daresay, but I'd like to know *this* reason. By the way, have you found out who the man is yet ? "

" Well, no. But there's been a police detective down, and I fancy he has an inkling of something. The rumour is that the poor chap was a Russian—used to travelling on the Siberian line, where there are few bridges, I should think."

"Can I see him ? "

" If you like. It's rather a gruesome sight. Come along."

He took Hazell to an office and unlocked the door.

" I'd rather not go in, if you don't mind," he said. " I've seen enough already, and I'm squeamish about these things."

Hazell nodded, and went up to the table where the dead man lay, covered with a sheet. He removed the sheet from his head, and looked carefully at the wound. Then he seemed satisfied, and rejoined his friend.

"Now," he said, "I want to have a look at the bridge itself. May I walk up the line?"

"Certainly, if you want the trouble. Stop a moment, though—there's a goods train just starting—you can have a lift in the brake, and I'll tell 'em to slow down for you to get off. But you'll have to walk back."

"All right. When's the inquest?"

"To-morrow."

When Hazell got off the goods brake he found a young man standing by the side of the line making a sketch of the bridge.

"Good-morning," said the latter. "Represent a paper?"

"No."

"Oh! I'm on the *Midland Courier*. We shall have a block in to-morrow. Terrible thing. Seen the bloodstains?"

He was very young at his work, and Hazell, with a slight smile at his impulsiveness, replied in the negative.

"Come along then, and I'll show them to you. They're quite plain. Got a bit frozen, and it hasn't thawed to-day."

He took Hazell some twenty or thirty yards beyond the bridge, and pointed out, on the frosty track, a few dark stains on the ballast and ends of the sleepers.

"Must have been killed instantly," he went on, garrulously. "I draw a bit, you see, so I'm making a sketch of the affair—just at the moment when he struck his head against the bridge."

"When he struck his head against the bridge,"

echoed Hazell, thoughtfully. "Well, don't let me interrupt you. Look out, young man, though, or there'll be a second accident!"

They had gone back to the up side of the bridge, and the young reporter was standing on the line. Hazell had heard a signal fall, and knew a train was coming. The other thanked him for his warning.

"Just what I wanted," he said. "I shall get an impression of the thing now."

Hazell carefully watched the train as it ran beneath the bridge. Then he shook his head, and muttered to himself:

"Just what I thought. He'd have to lean out a tremendous distance. And yet he must have been killed here. It's very strange."

Here he looked at his watch, eat a plasmon biscuit, and solemnly proceeded to go through an "exercise," for which purpose he took off his coat. Having finished his little performance he set to work to examine the edge of the brickwork. This proved unsatisfactory. Then his gaze fell on the metals as he stood, just at the entrance to the bridge, wrapped in thought.

Suddenly he appeared to catch sight of something on the line. The next moment he was down on his hands and knees beside the track. Close to the end of one of the sleepers, outside the left hand rail, he had noticed a hole. That was all. Nothing very curious, perhaps, but he knew very well that holes are never bored in such places.

This one had evidently been done with an auger, for a few shreds of wood were beside the sleeper, It was large enough for him to insert his little finger. and he felt that there was a thread inside. Something had been screwed into that hole.

"Found some more blood?" shouted the sanguinary-minded youth.

Hazell shook his head as he stood up and looked overhead. The sleeper with the hole in it was immediately below the edge of the bridge. He looked long and intently at the bridge, marking with his eyes an imaginary line straight up the brickwork from the hole in the sleeper.

Apparently unsatisfied, he found his way to the top of the bridge, and carefully examined the parapet. An exclamation of triumph escaped him. About a foot above the roadway an exceedingly strong staple had been driven into the brickwork, the fragments of dislodged mortar lying on the ground. He measured a straight line up from the staple to the top of the parapet, looked over, and found the line would drop exactly perpendicular to the hole in the sleeper. A careful examination of the staple revealed a tiny shred of tow attached to it.

He waited patiently till another train was signalled, and then, watching from the top of the parapet, he convinced himself that the imaginary perpendicular line down to the sleeper would just clear the sides of the carriages, as they ran by, by a few inches.

"Good!" he said. "I was certain it wasn't an accident."

He stood on the bridge, thinking, and taking in the surrounding country. A farmhouse and a few scattered cottages stood a little way back from the line and about a couple hundred yards from the bridge. One or two other houses were in the distance. Then he looked at the roadway, which was hard with the frost.

Suddenly he whistled softly to himself. There were tracks of a bicycle coming up the bridge. The machine had evidently been leaned against the parapet. And the rider had returned by the same road by which he had come. There was his second track frozen into the road, and not a sign of it on the other side of the bridge.

Few bicycles of any wear lack some distinguishing mark in the tyres, and Hazell was soon satisfied, after a little examination, that the ones in question were Clipper Reflex, and that a small bit had been chipped out of the back tyre, making its mark plainly in the road.

"How are you getting on?" he shouted to the reporter presently.

"Just finished."

"Where does this road lead to?"

"It's only a bye road, and not much used. But you can get back to Manningford by taking the first turning to the right. If you go straight on it leads to Sandfield."

"Thanks. Nice frosty morning for a walk. I say, do you happen to know when the frost set in in this part of the country?"

"Yes. It wasn't freezing at eight last night, when I went round to my office for some late work, but it was quite hard at ten or so when I came back."

"Thanks. Good morning."

"Good morning!"

"Well," said Hazell to himself, as he walked quickly away, "he was a clumsy beggar to ride a soft road. The whole thing's as plain as daylight, except just one point. How did he know the fellow would put his head out of the window just in the right place? There's a mystery in this, and I'd like to solve it before I say anything to the police. At present we'll try the only clue there seems to be."

The bicycle track did not branch off to Manning-ford, and Hazell traced it for over eight miles along the road to Sandfield. He broke the journey at a farmhouse, where he begged for a glass of milk and a dry crust of bread. When he had partaken of this he astonished the woman who had given it to him by lying down flat on his back and rubbing his chest violently; after which he gave her half-a-crown, and explained that "chest massage" was one of the best aids to digestion. As he drew near Sandfield it became difficult to follow the track, on account of the increased traffic, but the frost was his best friend, and he persistently recovered the traces.

At length they led him down a street on the out-skirts of the town, and stopped abruptly opposite a terrace of small houses. He waited a moment or two in hesitation, not being quite sure which house might prove the right one, and also wondering whether it were not his duty to go straight to the police and tell them his conjectures. But at that moment, a woman, who had been observing him through one of the windows, came to the door and accosted him.

" This is the house you're looking for, I think, sir ? "

He turned towards her in surprise.

" The young man's very ill, sir, and I thought I'd better send for you, me not knowin' anything about him, and feeling if so be as anything was to happen to him it wouldn't be right not to have no one to give a certificate, he bein' without friends, leastwise he *do* get letters, but when I asked him to send for someone as knows him he wouldn't hear of it, which I says I'd post a letter or even write it for him. But he's obstinate, though I told him I'd send for you, which they said you was out, sir, and would call when you came home."

The woman paused to take breath, and Hazell fell in with the situation.

"A lodger of yours, I suppose ?"

"Which he's only been with me a short time, and pays his rent reg'lar, sir, though he is, seemingly, a furriner, which I never could a-bear, sir, though he do speak the King's English quite as good as you nor me."

Hazell smiled at her idea of grammar, and asked casually as he went into the house :

"What's the matter with him ?"

"It ain't for me to say, sir ; but I lost a boy of my own with conjecture of the lungs and browntitis, and I know what the sympt:ms is, which he wouldn't take no care of hisself."

"Ah, been riding his bicycle in these cold east winds, eh ?" went on Hazell as his eyes fell on a machine in the hall.

"Only last night, sir, did he go out, which I told him was a-runnin' against Providence with his cough so bad as the neighbours could hear it over the street."

"Well, I'll go up and see him."

"Do so, sir—the first room on the left."

A sound of coughing struck upon his ears as he opened the door. On the bed lay a young man with fair hair, slight moustache, and hectic cheeks. He turned to Hazell and said feebly, and with a foreign accent :

"Ah, you are the doctor, I suppose. Mrs. Bull insisted on sending for you, but I'm afraid you can't do me very much good."

Hazell locked the door very quietly on the inside,

and came up to the head of the bed.

"I'm not the doctor," he began, "though your landlady mistook me for him."

The glow faded from the sick man's cheeks as he raised his head from the pillow. "Who—who are you?" he asked.

"I can hardly explain. I'm scarcely a detective, being only a private individual."

"What do you mean about being a detective?" gasped the other.

"I mean that somewhere in this room—unless you threw them away on the road—you have an auger, a hammer, a large staple with a screw, and a length of very strong rope."

"Good God!" exclaimed the sick man, "how did you find that out?"

"By your own clumsiness. It was a clever thing to stretch that rope from the bridge to the sleeper, but it was foolish to ride your bicycle there in the mud with a frost about to set in."

A violent fit of coughing seized the man for a minute or two. Hazell poured him out a drink of water, and looked at him critically.

"You are very ill," he said.

"I know I am. I don't expect to get over it. What are you going to do? Have me hanged if I live long enough?" he asked bitterly.

Hazell was silent.

"Perhaps you don't know who the man was who was found dead at Manningford last night?"

Hazell shook his head.

"Let me tell you before you do anything. You say you're not a detective, but I suppose you'll tell the police. I don't care. Murder, was it? No, no, no. It was a just judgment and punishment.

If ever a man deserved his fate he did.   Have you ever heard of Paul Gourchoff?"

"No."

"That was his name.   One of the cruellest and most bloodthirsty of all the Russian Police Agents, a man whose life was stained with the foulest crimes. Shall I tell you about him?"

Hazell nodded.

"I will—and then I'll leave the issue in your hands, and you can do as you please.   I am a Pole —yes, you can understand something of what I am by the mere word.   It is enough for a Pole to be loyal to his country and to labour for the cause of freedom, and then he becomes—if he is fortunate enough to escape Siberia, or prison, or death—an outcast, like myself.

"My father had a little estate; he was one of the old nobility—we are of the Radziwill family, and he plotted, secretly, as every patriot has to plot. This man, Gourchoff, was one of us, trusted with all our plans, but in the pay of the accursed Tsar all the time.

"He waited his opportunity, and then—well, I will spare you the details.   My father died on the way to Siberia, a brother and sister are there, somewhere, lost to name even—mere numbers, being slowly done to death.   One sister was killed before my eyes—a brutal cossack cut her down with his sword.   I was the only one of the family that escaped, and that by a miracle.

"This was five years ago, and since that time I have devoted my life to the cause here in England. There are many of us.   Some come over, secretly, from Poland, to keep in touch with those who work in our country.   We can do much here, but it is difficult.

" Two months ago a tremendous blow was struck at our organisation.   Paul Gourchoff came to England.   He is like a sleuth hound, and we knew that if he once tracked our meetings it would mean death or exile to many of our friends in Poland.

" Can you wonder that we determined to take strong measures ?   Can you wonder that *I* sought my opportunity for revenge ?   But he was wily. He knew the danger, and it was impossible at first to do anything, although every day he was discovering more and more and running us down.   Then I devised the plan which you seem to have fathomed. And it was successful.   Gourchoff is dead.   Bah ! "

Another fit of coughing succeeded.   Then Hazell asked :

" But how did you make him put his head out of that window just at the right spot ? "

" I am coming to that.   I came down here and took rooms, and he was allowed to find out that I was in the neighbourhocd.   That was the first step. His great plan was to discover the secret rendezvous where we met our compatriots who came over.

" That remains a secret still !

" But it was not in London, and he knew it.   So then we went to work carefully.   We had discovered that one of us, a man we had never really trusted, was in his pay.   Through this man we arranged that he should receive information, which we apparently allowed to leak out.   At first the disclosure was made to him that we met in a house somewhere near the London and Mid-Northern Railway in this locality.   This, of course, was false.

" Then we let it be known that our friends came to this rendezvous in various ways, and that signals were arranged to show them if it were safe.   He fell into the trap beautifully. So we led him to believe that a meeting was to be held last night, and that two of our number were going from London. Between Bridgeworth and Manningford they were to give a signal by holding a lantern out of the window for a moment. This signal was to be answered by a green light in the window of a certain house near the side of the line if all was well, by a red light if there was danger. These lights were to be flashed, and not stationary.

"Now we knew his object was simply to discover the house, with a view to a raid on some subsequent occasion—oh! you little know of the secret raids that are made by Russian police in England—so that he would journey down alone.

"Our two friends were to get in the back of the train, and of course he ·was to be allowed to see them get in. That insured that he should go towards the front, and crane his head out of the window between Bridgeworth and Manningford. We let it be thought that the flash should take place from a window at the *side* of the house, so that he would be looking back.

"Heaven knows how I managed that ride last night—it has put the finishing stroke to a long illness. I had taken the most careful measurements beforehand, and knew exactly where to drive the staple in the brickwork, and where to bore the hole in the sleeper. It didn't take me long to fix the rope very tightly—I had it loose till just before the train was due.

"As I stood on the top of the bridge I could see him with his head reached out dimly in the darkness, while one of our friends at the back was holding out a small lantern. I knew, by the sound, that the rope had caught him, and I saw the other man draw in his head quickly. I unscrewed the staple from the sleeper, but I couldn't draw the other from the brickwork.

"There—that is the whole story. To my certain knowledge, Paul Gourchoff has caused the death or exile of over two hundred men and women, whose sole crime was patriotism and love of freedom. Did he deserve to die?"

And Hazell, who had listened to the recital attentively, nodded his head slowly.

"I think he did," he said.

Presently he added:

"Can I do anything for you?"

"No," replied Radziwill. "I don't think any-one can do that. In your kindness you might leave me alone—that is all. I shall cheat the gallows. There is enough money in my clothes here to bury me. I have nothing to live for. Oh, do what you like!"

And he turned over and hid his face in the pillow. Hazell went downstairs. Mrs. Bull was talking to a gentleman at the door.

"Which it's very strange, sir, you bein' the doctor as was sent for, and yet another doctor's with him now, and——"

"I'll put that right," replied Hazell. "Your patient is waiting to see you, sir."

"Oh, I see. Are you a friend of his?"

"Ye-es," replied Hazell. "I'd like to know what you think of him, so I'll wait till you come down."

And what the doctor thought of him was this:

"He may last two or three days, but he won't see the week out."

So Thorpe Hazell kept silence. He asked the

doctor to direct him to a vegetarian restaurant, where he lunched on a rice pudding and a dish of prunes. Then he took the local train from Sandfield to Manningford, and saw Rolfe once more before returning to town.

"Well," said the superintendent, "are you satisfied with your investigation?"

"Quite," returned Hazell.

"Only an ordinary case, eh?"

"Only an ordinary case. I beg your pardon, Mr. Rolfe, but how much do you weigh?"

"Fourteen stone, I believe," replied the official, with a puzzled air.

"And you are about five feet six, I should imagine," went on Hazell, looking at him critically. "You really ought to reduce some of it. Try living on lentils for a fortnight; and a very excellent exercise is this—I do it before most meals—take three deep breaths through the nostrils, filling the lungs and letting the air escape through the mouth slowly. At the same time rise on the toes, reach the hands above the head, and bring them slowly down to the sides. Repeat fifteen times. It's a capital thing for digestion. Good-bye!"

Two days later came the result of the inquest. Verdict, "Accidental death, with a recommendation from the jury that the railway officials should carefully examine the width of all their bridges, and take steps, if necessary, to avoid the occurrence of such a painful tragedy."

III

THE AFFAIR OF THE CORRIDOR EXPRESS

THORPE HAZELL stood in his study in his London flat. On the opposite wall he had pinned a bit of paper, about an inch square, at the height of his eye, and was now going through the most extraordinary contortions.

With his eyes fixed on the paper he was craning his neck as far as it would reach and twisting his head about in all directions. This necessitated a fearful rolling of the eyes in order to keep them on the paper, and was supposed to be a means of strengthening the muscles of the eye for angular sight.

Presently there came a tap at the door.

" Come in! " cried Hazell, still whirling his head round.

" A gentleman wishes to see you at once, sir! " said the servant, handing him a card.

Hazell paused in his exercises, took it from the tray, and read:

" Mr. F. W. Wingrave, M.A., B.Sc."

"Oh, show him in," said Hazell, rather impatiently, for he hated to be interrupted when he was doing his " eye gymnastics."

There entered a young man of about five-and-twenty, with a look of keen anxiety on his face.

" You are Mr. Thorpe Hazell ? " he asked.

" I am."

" You will have seen my name on my card—I am one of the masters at Shillington School—I had heard your name, and they told me at the station that it might be well to consult you—I hope you don't mind—I know you're not an ordinary detective, but—— "

"Sit down, Mr. Wingrave," said Hazell, interrupting his nervous flow of language. " You look quite ill and tired."

"I have just been through a very trying experience," replied Wingrave, sinking into a seat. " A boy I was in charge of has just mysteriously disappeared, and I want you to find him for me, and I want to ask your opinion. They say you know all about railways, but—— "

"Now, look here, my dear sir, you just have some hot toast and water before you say another word. I conclude you want to consult me on some railway matter. I'll do what I can, but I won't hear you till you've had some refreshment. Perhaps you prefer whiskey—though I don't advise it."

Wingrave, however, chose the whiskey, and Hazell poured him out some, adding soda-water.

" Thank you," he said. " I hope you'll be able to give me advice. I am afraid the poor boy must be killed; the whole thing is a mystery, and I—— "

" Stop a bit, Mr. Wingrave. I must ask you to tell me the story from the very beginning. That's the best way."

"Quite right. The worry of it has made me incoherent, I fear. But I'll try and do what you propose. First of all, do you know the name of Carr-Mathers?"

"Yes, I think so. Very rich, is he not?"

"A millionaire. He has only one child, a boy of about ten, whose mother died at his birth. He is a small boy for his age, and idolised by his father. About three months ago this young Horace Carr-Mathers was sent to our school—Cragsbury House, just outside Shillington. It is not a very large school, but exceedingly select, and the headmaster, Dr. Spring, is well known in high-class circles. I may tell you that we have the sons of some of the leading nobility preparing for the public schools. You will readily understand that in such an establishment as ours the most scrupulous care is exercised over the boys, not only as regards their moral and intellectual training, but also to guard against any outside influences."

"Kidnapping, for example," interposed Hazell.

"Exactly. There have been such cases known, and Dr. Spring has a very high reputation to maintain. The slightest rumour against the school would go ill with him—and with all of us masters.

"Well, this morning the headmaster received a telegram about Horace Carr-Mathers, requesting that he should be sent up to town."

"Do you know the exact wording?" asked Hazell.

"I have it with me," replied Wingrave, drawing it from his pocket.

Hazell took it from him, and read as follows :

"*Please grant Horace leave of absence for two days. Send him to London by 5.45 express from Shillington, in first-class carriage, giving guard instructions to look after him. We will meet train in town.—Carr-Mathers.*"

"Um," grunted Hazell, as he handed it back. "Well, he can afford long telegrams."

"Oh, he's always wiring about something or other," replied Wingrave; "he seldom writes a letter. Well, when the doctor received this he called me into his study.

"'I suppose I must let the boy go,' he said, 'but I'm not at all inclined to allow him to travel by himself. If anything should happen to him his father would hold us responsible as well as the railway company. So you had better take him up to town, Mr. Wingrave.'

"'Yes, sir.'

"'You need do no more than deliver him to his father. If Mr. Carr-Mathers is not at the terminus to meet him, take him with you in a cab to his house in Portland Place. You'll probably be able to catch the last train home, but, if not, you can get a bed at an hotel.'

"'Very good, sir.'

"So, shortly after half-past five, I found myself standing on the platform at Shillington, waiting for the London express."

"Now, stop a moment," interrupted Hazell, sipping a glass of filtered water which he had poured out for himself. "I want to get a clear notion of this journey of yours from the beginning, for, I presume, you will shortly be telling me that something strange happened during it. Was there anything to be noticed before the train started?"

"Nothing at the time. But I remembered afterwards that two men seemed to be watching me rather closely when I took the tickets, and I heard one of them say 'Confound,' beneath his breath. But my suspicions were not aroused at the moment."

"I see. If there is anything in this it was probably because he was disconcerted when he saw you

were going to travel with the boy. Did these two
men get into the train?"

" I'm coming to that. The train was in sharp to
time, and we took our seats in a first-class compartment."

" Please describe the exact position."

" Our carriage was the third from the front. It
was a corridor train, with access from carriage to
carriage all the way through. Horace and myself
were in a compartment alone. I had bought him
some illustrated papers for the journey, and for some
time he sat quietly enough, looking through them.
After a bit he grew fidgety, as you know boys will."

" Wait a minute. I want to know if the corridor
of your carriage was on the left or on the right—
supposing you to be seated facing the engine?"

" On the left."

" Very well, go on."

" The door leading into the corridor stood open.
It was still daylight, but dusk was setting in fast—I
should say it was about half-past six, or a little more.
Horace had been looking out of the window on the
right side of the train when I drew his attention to
Rutherham Castle, which we were passing. It
stands, as you know, on the left side of the line. In
order to get a better view of it he went out into the
corridor and stood there. I retained my seat on the
right side of the compartment, glancing at him from
time to time. He seemed interested in the corridor
itself, looking about him, and once or twice shutting
and opening the door of our compartment. I can
see now that I ought to have kept a sharper eye on
him, but I never dreamed that any accident could
happen. I was reading a paper myself, and became
rather interested in a paragraph. It may have been

seven or eight minutes before I looked up. When I did so, Horace had disappeared.

"I didn't think anything of it at first, but only concluded that he had taken a walk along the corridor."

"You don't know which way he went?" inquired Hazell.

"No. I couldn't say. I waited a minute or two, and then rose and looked out into the corridor. There was no one there. Still my suspicions were not aroused. It was possible that he had gone to the lavatory. So I sat down again, and waited. Then I began to get a little anxious, and determined to have a look for him. I walked to either end of the corridor, and searched the lavatories, but they were both empty. Then I looked in all the other compartments of the carriage, and asked their occupants if they had seen him go by, but none of them had noticed him."

"Do you remember how these compartments were occupied?"

"Yes. In the first, which was reserved for ladies, there were five ladies. The next was a smoker with three gentlemen in it. Ours came next. Then, going towards the front of the train, were the two men I had noticed at Shillington; the last compartment had a gentleman and lady and their three children."

"Ah! how about those two men—what were they doing?"

"One of them was reading a book, and the other appeared to be asleep."

"Tell me. Was the door leading to the corridor from their compartment shut?"

"Yes, it was."

" Go on."

" Well, I was in a most terrible fright, and I went back to my compartment and pulled the electric communicator.   In a few seconds the front guard came along the corridor and asked me what I wanted.   I told him I had lost my charge. He suggested that the boy had walked through to another carriage, and I asked him if he would mind my making a thorough search of the train with him.   To this he readily agreed.   We went back to the first carriage and began to do so.   We examined every compartment from end to end of the train ; we looked under every seat, in spite of the protestations of some of the passengers ; we searched all the lavatories— every corner of the train—and we found absolutely no trace of Horace Carr-Mathers.   No one had seen the boy anywhere."

" Had the train stopped ? "

" Not for a second.   It was going at full speed all the time.   It only slowed down after we had finished the search—but it never quite stopped."

" Ah !   We'll come to that presently.   I want to ask you some questions first. Was it still daylight ? "

" Dusk, but quite light enough to see plainly— besides which, the train lamps were lit."

" Exactly.   Those two men, now, in the next compartment to yours—tell me precisely what happened when you visited them the second time with the guard."

" They asked a lot of questions—like many of the other passengers—and seemed very surprised."

" You looked underneath their seats ? "

" Certainly."

" On the luggage-racks ?   A small boy like that could be rolled up in a rug and put on the rack."

" We examined every rack on the train."

Thorpe Hazell lit a cigarette and smoked furiously, motioning to his companion to keep quiet. He was thinking out the situation. Suddenly he said:

" How about the window in those two men's compartment ? "

" It was shut—I particularly noticed it."

" You are *quite sure* you searched the whole of the train ? "

" Absolutely certain; so was the guard."

" Ah ! " remarked Hazell, " even guards are mistaken sometimes. It—er—was only the inside of the train you searched, eh ? "

" Of course."

" Very well," replied Hazell, " now, before we go any further, I want to ask you this. Would it have been to anyone's interest to have murdered the boy ? "

" I don't think so—from what I know. I don't see how it could be."

" Very well. We will take it as a pure case of kidnapping, and presume that he is alive and well. This ought to console you to begin with."

" Do you think you can help me ? "

" I don't know yet. But go on and tell me all that happened."

" Well, after we had searched the train I was at my wits' end—and so was the guard. We both agreed, however, that nothing more could be done till we reached London. Somehow, my strongest suspicions concerning those two men were aroused, and I travelled in their compartment for the rest of the journey."

" Oh ! Did anything happen ? "

" Nothing. They both wished me good-night,

hoped I'd find the boy, got out, and drove off in a hansom."

" And then ? "

" I looked about for Mr. Carr-Mathers, but he was nowhere to be seen. Then I saw an inspector, and put the case before him. He promised to make inquiries and to have the line searched on the part where I missed Horace. I took a hansom to Portland Place, only to discover that Mr. Carr-Mathers is on the Continent and not expected home for a week. Then I came on to you—the inspector had advised me to do so. And that's the whole story. It's a terrible thing for me, Mr. Hazell. What do you think of it ? "

" Well," replied Hazell, " of course it's very clear that there is a distinct plot. Someone sent that telegram, knowing Mr. Carr-Mathers' proclivities. The object was to kidnap the boy. It sounds absurd to talk of brigands and ransoms in this country, but the thing is done over and over again for all that. It is obvious that the boy was expected to travel alone, and that the train was the place chosen for the kidnapping. Hence the elaborate directions. I think you were quite right in suspecting those two men, and it might have been better if you had followed them up without coming to me."

" But they went off alone ! "

" Exactly. It's my belief they had originally intended doing so after disposing of Horace, and that they carried out their original intentions."

" But what became of the boy ?—how did they——"

" Stop a bit. I'm not at all clear in my own mind. But you mentioned that while you were concluding your search with the guard the train slackened speed ? "

" Yes. It almost came to a stop—and then went very slowly for a minute or so. I asked the guard why, but I didn't understand his reply."

" What was it ? "

" He said it was a P.W. operation."

Hazell laughed.

" P.W. stands for permanent way," he explained, " I know exactly what you mean now. There is a big job going on near Longmoor—they are raising the level of the line, and the up-trains are running on temporary rails. So they have to proceed very slowly. Now it was after this that you went back to the two men whom you suspected ? "

" Yes."

" Very well. Now let me think the thing over. Have some more whiskey? You might also like to glance at the contents of my book-case. If you know anything of first editions and bindings they will interest you."

Wingrave, it is to be feared, paid but small heed to the books, but watched Hazell anxiously as the latter smoked cigarette after cigarette, his brows knit in deep thought. After a bit he said slowly:

" You will understand that I am going to work upon the theory that the boy has been kidnapped and that the original intention has been carried out, in spite of the accident of your presence in the train. How the boy was disposed of meanwhile is what baffles me; but that is a detail—though it will be interesting to know how it was done. Now, I don't want to raise any false hopes, because I may very likely be wrong, but we are going to take action upon a very feasible assumption, and if I am at all correct, I hope to put you definitely on the track. Mind, I don't promise to do so, and, at best, I don't promise to do *more* than put you on a track. Let me see—it's just after nine. We have plenty of time. We'll drive first to Scotland Yard, for it will be as well to have a detective with us."

He filled a flask with milk, put some plasmon biscuits and a banana into a sandwich case, and then ordered his servant to hail a cab.

An hour later, Hazell, Wingrave, and a man from Scotland Yard were closeted together in one of the private offices of the Mid-Eastern Railway with one of the chief officials of the line. The latter was listening attentively to Hazell.

" But I can't understand the boy not being any-where in the train, Mr. Hazell," he said.

" I can—partly," replied Hazell, " but first let me see if my theory is correct."

" By all means. There's a down-train in a few minutes. I'll go with you, for the matter is very interesting. Come along, gentlemen."

He walked forward to the engine and gave a few instructions to the driver, and then they took their seats in the train. After a run of half an hour or so they passed a station.

" That's Longmoor," said the official, " now we shall soon be on the spot. It's about a mile down that the line is being raised."

Hazell put his head out of the window. Presently an ominous red light showed itself. The train came almost to a stop, and then proceeded slowly, the man who had shown the red light changing it to green. They could see him as they passed, standing close to a little temporary hut. It was his duty to warn all approaching drivers, and for this purpose

he was stationed some three hundred yards in front
of the bit of line that was being operated upon.
Very soon they were passing this bit. Naphtha
lamps shed a weird light over a busy scene, for the
work was being continued night and day. A score
or so of sturdy navvies were shovelling and picking
along the track.

Once more into the darkness. On the other side
of the scene of operations, at the same distance,
was another little hut, with a guardian for the up-
train. Instead of increasing the speed in passing
this hut, which would have been usual, the driver
brought the train almost to a standstill. As he did
so the four men got out of the carriage, jumping
from the footboard to the ground. On went the
train, leaving them on the left side of the down track,
just opposite the little hut. They could see the
man standing outside, his back partly turned to
them. There was a fire in a brazier close by that
dimly outlined his figure.

He started suddenly, as they crossed the line
towards him.

"What are you doing here?" he cried. "You've
no business here—you're trespassing."

He was a big, strong-looking man, and he backed
a little towards his hut as he spoke.

"I am Mr. Mills, the assistant-superintendent of
the line," replied the official, coming forward.

"Beg pardon, sir; but how was I to know that?"
growled the man.

"Quite right. It's your duty to warn off
strangers. How long have you been stationed
here?"

"I came on at five o'clock; I'm regular night-
watchman, sir."

"Ah! Pretty comfortable, eh?"

"Yes, thank you, sir," replied the man, wondering why the question was asked, but thinking, not unnaturally, that the assistant-superintendent had come down with a party of engineers to inspect things.

"Got the hut to yourself?"

"Yes, sir."

Without another word, Mr. Mills walked to the door of the hut. The man, his face suddenly growing pale, moved, and stood with his back to it.

"It's—it's private, sir!" he growled.

Hazell laughed.

"All right, my man," he said. "I was right, I think—hullo!—look out! Don't let him go!"

For the man had made a quick rush forward. But the Scotland Yard officer and Hazell were on him in a moment, and a few seconds later the handcuffs clicked on his wrists. Then they flung the door open, and there, lying in the corner, gagged and bound, was Horace Carr-Mathers.

An exclamation of joy broke forth from Wingrave, as he opened his knife to cut the cords. But Hazell stopped him.

"Just half a moment," he said: "I want to see how they've tied him up."

A peculiar method had been adopted in doing this. His wrists were fastened behind his back, a stout cord was round his body just under the arm-pits, and another cord above the knees. These were connected by a slack bit of rope.

"All right!" went on Hazell; "let's get the poor lad out of his troubles—there, that's better. How do you feel, my boy?"

"Awfully stiff!" said Horace, "but I'm not hurt.

I say, sir," he continued to Wingrave, "how did you know I was here. I *am* glad you've come."

" The question is how did you *get* here ? " replied Wingrave. " Mr. Hazell, here, seemed to know where you were, but it's a puzzle to me at present."

" If you'd come half an hour later you wouldn't have found him," growled the man who was hand-cuffed. " I ain't so much to blame as them as employed me."

" Oh, is that how the land lies ? " exclaimed Hazell. " I see. You shall tell us presently, my boy, how it happened. Meanwhile, Mr. Mills, I think we can prepare a little trap—eh ? "

In five minutes all was arranged. A couple of the navvies were brought up from the line, one stationed outside to guard against trains, and with certain other instructions, the other being inside the hut with the rest of them. A third navvy was also dispatched for the police.

" How are they coming ? " asked Hazell of the handcuffed man.

" They were going to take a train down from London to Rockhampstead on the East-Northern, and drive over. It's about ten miles off."

" Good ! they ought soon to be here," replied Hazell, as he munched some biscuits and washed them down with a draught of milk, after which he astonished them all by solemnly going through one of his " digestive exercises."

A little later they heard the sound of wheels on a road beside the line. Then the man on watch said, in gruff tones :

" The boy's inside ! "

But they found more than the boy inside, and an

hour later all three conspirators were safely lodged in Longmoor gaol.

" Oh, it was awfully nasty, I can tell you," said Horace Carr-Mathers, as he explained matters afterwards. " I went into the corridor, you know, and was looking about at things, when all of a sudden I felt my coat-collar grasped behind, and a hand was laid over my mouth. I tried to kick and shout, but it was no go. They got me into the compartment, stuffed a handkerchief into my mouth, and tied it in. It was just beastly. Then they bound me hand and foot, and opened the window on the right-hand side—opposite the corridor. I was in a funk, for I thought they were going to throw me out, but one of them told me to keep my pecker up, as they weren't going to hurt me. Then they let me down out of the window by that slack rope, and made it fast to the handle of the door outside. It was pretty bad. There was I, hanging from the door-handle in a sort of doubled-up position, my back resting on the footboard of the carriage, and the train rushing along like mad. I felt sick and awful, and I had to shut my eyes. I seemed to hang there for ages."

" I told you you only examined the *inside* of the train," said Thorpe Hazell to Wingrave. " I had my suspicions that he was somewhere on the outside all the time, but I was puzzled to know where. It was a clever trick."

" Well," went on the boy, " I heard the window open above me after a bit. I looked up and saw one of the men taking the rope off the handle. The train was just beginning to slow down. Then he hung out of the window, dangling me with one hand. It was horrible. I was hanging below the footboard now. Then the train came almost to a stop, and someone caught me round the waist. I lost my senses for a minute or two, and then I found myself lying in the hut."

" Well, Mr. Hazell," said the assistant-superintendent, " you were perfectly right, and we all owe you a debt of gratitude."

" Oh ! " said Hazell, " it was only a guess at the best. I presumed it was simply kidnapping, and the problem to be solved was how and where the boy was got off the train without injury. It was obvious that he had been disposed of before the train reached London. There was only one other inference. The man on duty was evidently the confederate, for, if not, his presence would have stopped the whole plan of action. I'm very glad to have been of any use. There are interesting points about the case, and it has been a pleasure to me to undertake it."

A little while afterwards Mr. Carr-Mathers himself called on Hazell to thank him.

" I should like," he said, " to express my deep gratitude substantially; but I understand you are not an ordinary detective. But is there any way in which I can serve you, Mr. Hazell ? "

" Yes—two ways."

" Please name them."

" I should be sorry for Mr. Wingrave to get into trouble through this affair—or Dr. Spring either."

" I understand you, Mr. Hazell. They were both to blame, in a way. But I will see that Dr. Spring's reputation does not suffer, and that Wingrave comes out of it harmlessly."

" Thank you very much."

"You said there was a second way in which I could serve you."

"So there is. At Dunn's sale last month you were the purchaser of two first editions of 'The New Bath Guide.' If you cared to dispose of one, I——"

"Say no more, Mr. Hazell. I shall be glad to give you one for your collection."

Hazell stiffened.

"You misunderstand me!" he exclaimed icily. "I was about to add that if you cared to dispose of a copy I would write you out a cheque."

"Oh, certainly," replied Mr. Carr-Mathers with a smile, "I shall be extremely pleased."

Whereupon the transaction was concluded.

IV

SIR GILBERT MURRELL'S PICTURE

THE affair of the goods truck on the Didcot and Newbury branch of the Great Western Railway was of singular interest, and found a prominent place in Thorpe Hazell's notebook. It was owing partly to chance, and partly to Hazell's sagacity, that the main incidents in the story were discovered, but he always declared that the chief interest to his mind was the unique method by which a very daring plan was carried out.

He was staying with a friend at Newbury at the time, and had taken his camera down with him, for he was a bit of an amateur photographer as well as book-lover, though his photos generally consisted of trains and engines. He had just come in from a morning's ramble with his camera slung over his shoulder, and was preparing to partake of two plasmon biscuits, when his friend met him in the hall.

"I say, Hazell," he began, "you're just the fellow they want here."

"What's up?" asked Hazell, taking off his camera and commencing some "exercises."

"I've just been down to the station. I know the station-master very well, and he tells me an awfully queer thing happened on the line last night."

" Where ? "

" On the Didcot branch. It's a single line, you know, running through the Berkshire Downs to Didcot."

Hazell smiled, and went on whirling his arms round his head.

"Kind of you to give me the information," he said, "but I happen to know the line. But what's occurred ? "

" Well, it appears a goods train left Didcot last night bound through to Winchester, and that one of the waggons never arrived here at Newbury."

" Not very much in that," replied Hazell, still at his " exercises," "unless the waggon in question was behind the brake and the couplings snapped, in which case the next train along might have run into it."

" Oh, no. The waggon was in the middle of the train."

" Probably left in a siding by mistake," replied Hazell.

" But the station-master says that all the stations along the line have been wired to, and that it isn't at any of them."

" Very likely it never left Didcot."

" He declares there is no doubt about that."

" Well, you begin to interest me," replied Hazell, stopping his whirligigs and beginning to eat his plasmon. "There may be something in it, though very often a waggon is mislaid. But I'll go down to the station."

" I'll go with you, Hazell, and introduce you to the station-master. He has heard of your reputation."

Ten minutes later they were in the station-master's office, Hazell having re-slung his camera.

" Very glad to meet you," said that functionary, " for this affair promises to be mysterious. *I* can't make it out at all."

" Do you know what the truck contained ? "

" That's just where the bother comes in, sir. It was valuable property. There's a loan exhibition of pictures at Winchester next week, and this waggon was bringing down some of them from Leamington. They belong to Sir Gilbert Murrell—three of them, I believe—large pictures, and each in a separate packing-case."

" H'm—this sounds very funny. Are you *sure* the truck was on the train ? "

" Simpson, the brakesman, is here now, and I'll send for him. Then you can hear the story in his own words."

So the goods guard appeared on the scene. Hazell looked at him narrowly, but there was nothing suspicious in his honest face.

" I know the waggon was on the train when we left Didcot," he said in answer to inquiries, " and I noticed it at Upton, the next station, where we took a couple off. It was the fifth or sixth in front of my brake. I'm quite certain of that. We stopped at Compton to take up a cattle truck, but I didn't get out there. Then we ran right through to Newbury, without stopping at the other stations, and then I discovered that the waggon was not on the train. I thought very likely it might have been left at Upton or Compton by mistake, but I was wrong, for they say it isn't there. That's all I know about it, sir. A rum go, ain't it ? "

3—Stories of the Railway.

"Extraordinary!" exclaimed Hazell. "You must have made a mistake."

"No, sir, I'm sure I haven't."

"Did the driver of the train notice anything?"

"No, sir."

"Well, but the thing's impossible," said Hazell. "A loaded waggon couldn't have been spirited away. What time was it when you left Didcot?"

"About eight o'clock, sir."

"Ah—quite dark. You noticed nothing along the line?"

"Nothing, sir."

"You were in your brake all the time, I suppose?"

"Yes, sir—while we were running."

At this moment there came a knock at the station-master's door and a porter entered.

"There's a passenger train just in from the Didcot branch," said the man, "and the driver reports that he saw a truck loaded with packing-cases in Churn siding."

"Well, I'm blowed!" exclaimed the brakesman. "Why, we ran through Churn without a stop—trains never do stop there except in camp time."

"Where is Churn?" asked Hazell, for once at a loss.

"It's merely a platform and a siding close to the camping ground between Upton and Compton," replied the station-master, "for the convenience of troops only, and very rarely used except in the summer, when soldiers are encamped there." *

"I should very much like to see the place, and as soon as possible," said Hazell.

---

* The incident here recorded occurred before June, 1905, in which month Churn was dignified with a place in *Bradshaw* as a 'station" at which trains stop by signal.—V. L. W.

" So you shall," replied the station-master. " A train will soon start on the branch. Inspector Hill shall go with you, and instruction shall be given to the driver to stop there, while a return train can pick you both up."

In less than an hour Hazell and Inspector Hill alighted at Churn. It is a lonely enough place, situated in a vast flat basin of the Downs, scarcely relieved by a single tree, and far from all human habitation with the exception of a lonely shepherd's cottage some half a mile away.

The " station " itself is only a single platform, with a shelter and a solitary siding, terminating in what is known in railway language as a " dead end " —that is, in this case, wooden buffers to stop any trucks. This siding runs off from the single line of rail at points from the Didcot direction of the line.

And in this siding was the lost truck, right against the " dead end," filled with three packing-cases, and labelled " Leamington to Winchester, *via* Newbury." There could be no doubt about it at all. But how it had got there from the middle of a train running through without a stop was a mystery even to the acute mind of Thorpe Hazell.

" Well," said the inspector when they had gazed long enough at the truck ; " we'd better have a look at the points. Come along."

There is not even a signal-box at this primitive station. The points are actuated by two levers in a ground frame, standing close by the side of the line, one lever unlocking and the other shifting the same points.

" How about these points ? " said Hazell as they drew near. " You only use them so occasionally, that I suppose they are kept out of action ? "

"Certainly," replied the inspector, "a block of wood is bolted down between the end of the point rail and the main rail, fixed as a wedge—ah! there it is, you see, quite untouched; and the levers themselves are locked—here's the keyhole in the ground frame. This is the strangest thing I've ever come across, Mr. Hazell."

Thorpe Hazell stood looking at the points and levers sorely puzzled. They *must* have been worked to get that truck in the siding, he knew well. But how?

Suddenly his face lit up. Oil evidently had been used to loosen the nut of the bolt that fixed the wedge of wood. Then his eyes fell on the handle of one of the two levers, and a slight exclamation of joy escaped him.

"Look," said the inspector at that moment, "it's impossible to pull them off," and he stretched out his hand towards a lever. To his astonishment Hazell seized him by the collar and dragged him back before he could touch it.

"I beg your pardon," he exclaimed, "hope I've not hurt you, but I want to photograph those levers first, if you don't mind."

The inspector watched him rather sullenly as he fixed his camera on a folding tripod stand he had with him, only a few inches from the handle of one of the levers, and took two very careful photographs of it.

"Can't see the use of that, sir," growled the inspector. But Hazell vouchsafed no reply.

"Let him find it out for himself," he thought.

Then he said aloud :

"I fancy they must have had that block out, inspector—and it's evident the points must have

been set to get the truck where it is. How it was
done is a problem, but if the doer of it was anything of a regular criminal, I think we might find
him."

"How ?" asked the puzzled inspector.

"Ah," was the response, " I'd rather not say at
present. Now, I should very much like to know
whether those pictures are intact ? "

"We shall soon find that out," replied the inspector, "for we'll take the truck back with us."
And he commenced undoing the bolt with a spanner,
after which he unlocked the levers.

" H'm—they work pretty freely," he remarked as
he pulled one.

"Quite so," said Hazell, "they've been oiled
recently."

There was an hour or so before the return train
would pass, and Hazell occupied it by walking to
the shepherd's cottage.

" I am hungry," he explained to the woman there,
"and hunger is Nature's dictate for food. Can you
oblige me with a couple cf onions and a broomstick ? "

And she talks to-day of the strange man who
"kept a swingin' o' that there broomstick round 'is
'ead and then eat them onions as solemn as a
judge."

The first thing Hazell did on returning to Newbury was to develop his photographs. The plates
were dry enough by the evening for him to print
one or two photos on gaslight-paper and to enclose
the clearest of them with a letter to a Scotland Yard
official whom he knew, stating that he would call
for an answer, as he intended returning to town in

a couple of days. The following evening he received a note from the station-master, which read—

DEAR SIR,

I promised to let you know if the pictures in the cases on that truck were in any way tampered with. I have just received a report from Winchester by which I understand that they have been unpacked and carefully examined by the Committee of the Loan Exhibition. The Committee are perfectly satisfied that they have not been damaged or interfered with in any way, and that they have been received just as they left the owner's hands.

We are still at a loss to account for the running of the waggon on to Churn siding or for the object in doing so. An official has been down from Paddington, and, at his request, we are not making the affair public—the goods having arrived in safety. I am sure you will observe confidence in this matter.

" More mysterious than ever," said Hazell to himself. " I can't understand it at all."

The next day he called at Scotland Yard and saw the official.

" I've had no difficulty with your little matter, you'll be glad to hear," he said. " We looked up our records and very soon spotted your man."

" Who is he ? "

" His real name is Edgar Jeffreys, but we know him under several aliases. He's served four sentences for burglary and robbery—the latter, a daring theft from a train, so he's in your line, Mr. Hazell. What's he been up to, and how did you get that print ? "

" Well," replied Hazell, " I don't quite know yet what he's been doing. But I should like to be able to find him if anything turns up. Never mind how I got the print—the affair is quite a private one at present, and nothing may come of it."

The official wrote an address on a bit of paper and handed it to Hazell.

"He's living there just now, under the name of Allen. We keep such men in sight, and I'll let you know if he moves."

When Hazell opened his paper the following morning he gave a cry of joy. And no wonder, for this is what he saw:

MYSTERY OF A PICTURE.

Sir Gilbert Murrell and the Winchester Loan Exhibition.

An Extraordinary Charge.

The Committee of the Loan Exhibition of Pictures to be opened next week at Winchester are in a state of very natural excitement brought about by a strange charge that has been made against them by Sir Gilbert Murrell.

Sir Gilbert, who lives at Leamington, is the owner of several very valuable pictures, among them being the celebrated "Holy Family," by Velasquez. This picture, with two others, was dispatched by him from Leamington to be exhibited at Winchester, and yesterday he journeyed to that city in order to make himself satisfied with the hanging arrangements, as he had particularly stipulated that "The Holy Family" was to be placed in a prominent position.

The picture in question was standing on the floor of the gallery, leaning against a pillar, when Sir Gilbert arrived with some representatives of the Committee.

Nothing occurred till he happened to walk behind the canvas, when he astounded those present by saying that the picture was not his at all, declaring that a copy had been substituted, and stating that he was absolutely certain on account of certain private marks of his at the back of the canvas which were quite indecipherable, and which were now missing. He admitted that the painting itself in every way resembled his picture, and that it was the cleverest forgery he had ever seen; but a very painful scene took place, the hanging committee stating that the picture had been received by them from the railway company just as it stood.

At present the whole affair is a mystery, but Sir Gilbert insisted most emphatically to our correspondent, who was able to see him, that the picture was certainly not his, and said that as the original is extremely valuable he intends holding the Committee responsible for the substitution which, he declares, has taken place.

It was evident to Hazell that the papers had not, as yet, got hold of the mysterious incident at Churn. As a matter of fact, the railway company had kept that affair strictly to themselves, and the loan committee knew nothing of what had happened on the line.

But Hazell saw that inquiries would be made, and determined to probe the mystery without delay. He saw at once that if there was any truth in Sir Gilbert's story the substitution had taken place in that lonely siding at Churn. He was staying at his London flat, and five minutes after he had read the paragraph had called a hansom and was being hurried off to a friend of his who was well known in art circles as a critic and art historian.

"I can tell you exactly what you want to know," said he, "for I've only just been looking it up, so as to have an article in the evening papers on it. There was a famous copy of the picture of Velasquez, said to have been painted by a pupil of his, and for some years there was quite a controversy among the respective owners as to which was the genuine one—just as there is to-day about a Madonna belonging to a gentleman at St. Moritz, but which a Vienna gallery also claims to possess.

"However, in the case of 'The Holy Family,' the dispute was ultimately settled once and for all years ago, and undoubtedly Sir Gilbert Murrell held the genuine picture. What became of the copy no one knows. For twenty years all trace of it has been lost. There—that's all I can tell you. I shall pad it out a bit in my article, and I must get to work on it at once. Good-bye!"

"One moment—where was the copy last seen?"

"Oh! the old Earl of Ringmere had it last, but when he knew it to be a forgery he is said to have sold it for a mere song, all interest in it being lost, you see."

"Let me see, he's a very old man, isn't he?"

"Yes—nearly eighty—a perfect enthusiast on pictures still, though."

"Only *said* to have sold it," muttered Hazell to himself, as he left the house; "that's very vague—and there's no knowing what these enthusiasts will do when they're really bent on a thing. Sometimes they lose all sense of honesty. I've known fellows actually rob a friend's collection of stamps or butter-flies. What if there's something in it? By George, what an awful scandal there would be! It seems to me that if such a scandal were prevented I'd be thanked all round. Anyhow, I'll have a shot at it on spec. And I *must* find out how that truck was run off the line."

When once Hazell was on the track of a railway mystery he never let a moment slip by. In an hour's time, he was at the address given him at Scotland Yard. On his way there he took a card from his case, a blank one, and wrote on it, " From the Earl of Ringmere." This he put into an envelope.

" It's a bold stroke," he said to himself, " but, if there's anything in it, it's worth trying."

So he asked for Allen. The woman who opened the door looked at him suspiciously, and said she didn't think Mr. Allen was in.

" Give him this envelope," replied Hazell. In a couple of minutes she returned, and asked him to follow her.

A short, wiry-looking man, with sharp, evil-looking eyes, stood in the room waiting for him and looking at him suspiciously.

" Well," he snapped, " what is it—what do you want ? "

" I come on behalf of the Earl of Ringmere. You will know that when I mention Churn," replied Hazell, playing his trump card boldly.

" Well," went on the man, " what about that ? "

Hazell wheeled round, locked the door suddenly, put the key in his pocket, and then faced his man. The latter darted forward, but Hazell had a revolver pointing at him in a twinkling.

" You——detective ! "

" No, I'm not—I told you I came on behalf of the Earl—that looks like hunting up matters for his sake, doesn't it ? "

" What does the old fool mean ? " asked Jeffreys.

" Oh ! I see you know all about it. Now listen to me quietly, and you may come to a little reason. You changed that picture at Churn the other night."

" You seem to know a lot about it," sneered the other, but less defiantly.

" Well, I do—but not quite all. You were foolish to leave your traces on that lever, eh ? "

" How did I do that ? " exclaimed the man, giving himself away.

" You'd been dabbling about with oil, you see, and you left your thumb-print on the handle. I photographed it, and they recognised it at Scotland Yard. Quite simple."

Jeffreys swore beneath his breath.

" I wish you'd tell me what you mean," he said.

" Certainly. I expect you've been well paid for this little job."

" If I have, I'm not going to take any risks. I told the old man so. He's worse than I am—he put me up to getting the picture. Let him take his chance when it comes out—I suppose he wants to keep his name out of it, that's why you're here."

" You're not quite right. Now just listen to me. You're a villain, and you deserve to suffer; but I'm acting in a purely private capacity, and I fancy if I can get the original picture back to its owner that it will be better for all parties to hush this affair up. Has the old Earl got it ? "

" No, not yet," admitted the other, " he was too artful. But he knows where it is, and so do I."

" Ah—now you're talking sense ! Look here ! You make a clean breast of it, and I'll take it down on paper. You shall swear to the truth of your statement before a commissioner for oaths—he need not see the actual confession. I shall hold this in case it is necessary ; but if you help me to get the picture back to Sir Gilbert, I don't think it will be."

After a little more conversation, Jeffreys explained. Before he did so, however, Hazell had taken a bottle of milk and a hunch of wholemeal bread from his pocket, and calmly proceeded to perform "exercises" and then to eat his "lunch," while Jeffreys told the following story:

"It was the old Earl who did it. How he got hold of me doesn't matter—perhaps I got hold of him—maybe I put him up to it—but that's not the question. He'd kept that forged picture of his in a lumber room for years, but he always had his eye on the genuine one. He paid a long price for the forgery, and he got to think that he *ought* to have the original. But there, he's mad on pictures.

"Well, as I say, he kept the forgery out of sight and let folks think he'd sold it, but all the time he was in hopes of getting it changed somehow for the original.

"Then I came along and undertook the job for him. There were three of us in it, for it was a ticklish business. We found out by what train the picture was to travel—that was easy enough. I got hold of a key to unlock that ground frame, and the screwing off of the bolt was a mere nothing. I oiled the points well, so that the thing should work as I wanted it to.

"One pal was with me—in the siding, ready to clap on the side brake when the truck was running in. I was to work the points, and my other pal, who had the most awkward job of all, was on the goods train—under a tarpaulin in a truck. He had two lengths of very stout rope with a hook at each end of them.

"When the train left Upton, he started his job. Goods trains travel very slowly, and there was plenty of time. Counting from the back brake van, the truck we wanted to run off was No. 5. First he hooked No. 4 truck to No. 6—fixing the hook at the side of the end of both trucks, and having the slack in his hand, coiled up.

"Then when the train ran down a bit of a decline he uncoupled No. 5 from No. 4—standing on No. 5 to do it. That was easy enough, for he'd taken a coupling staff with him ; then he paid out the slack till it was tight. Next he hooked his second rope from No. 5 to No. 6, uncoupled No. 5 from No. 6, and paid out the slack of the second rope.

"Now you can see what happened. The last few trucks of the train were being drawn by a long rope reaching from No. 4 to No. 6, and leaving a space in between. In the middle of this space No. 5 ran, drawn by a short rope from No. 6. My pal stood on No. 6, with a sharp knife in his hand.

"The rest was easy. I held the lever, close by the side of the line—coming forward to it as soon as the engine passed. The instant the space appeared after No. 6 I pulled it over, and No. 5 took the siding points, while my pal cut the rope at the same moment.

"Directly the truck had run by and off I reversed the lever so that the rest of the train following took the main line. There is a decline before Compton, and the last four trucks came running down to the main body of the train, while my pal hauled in the slack and finally coupled No. 4 to No. 6 when they came together. He jumped from the train as it ran very slowly into Compton. That's how it was done."

Hazell's eyes sparkled.

"It's the cleverest thing I've heard of on the line," he said.

"Think so? Well, it wanted some handling. The next thing was to unscrew the packing-case, take the picture out of the frame, and put the forgery we'd brought with us in its place. That took us some time, but there was no fear of interruption in that lonely part. Then I took the picture off, rolling it up first, and hid it. The old Earl insisted on this. I was to tell him where it was, and he was going to wait for a few weeks and then get it himself."

" Where did you hide it ? "

" You're sure you're going to hush this up ? "

" You'd have been in charge long ago if I were not."

" Well, there's a path from Churn to East Ilsley across the downs, and on the right-hand of that path is an old sheep well—quite dry. It's down there. You can easily find the string if you look for it—fixed near the top."

Hazell took down the man's confession, which was duly attested. His conscience told him that perhaps he ought to have taken stronger measures.

*　　　*　　　*　　　*　　　*

" I told you I was merely a private individual," said Hazell to Sir Gilbert Murrell. "I have acted in a purely private capacity in bringing you your picture."

Sir Gilbert looked from the canvas to the calm face of Hazell.

" Who are you, sir ? " he asked.

" Well, I rather aspire to be a book-collector ; you may have read my little monogram on " Jacobean Bindings ? "

" No," said Sir Gilbert, " I have not had that pleasure. But I must inquire further into this. How did you get this picture ? Where was it—who——"

" Sir Gilbert," broke in Hazell, " I could tell you

the whole truth, of course. I am not in any way to blame myself. By chance, as much as anything else, I discovered how your picture had been stolen, and where it was."

"But I want to know all about it. I shall prosecute—I——"

"I think not. Now, do you remember where the forged picture was seen last?"

"Yes; the Earl of Ringmere had it—he sold it."

"Did he?"

"Eh?"

"What if he kept it all this time?" said Hazell, with a peculiar look.

There was a long silence.

"Good heavens!" exclaimed Sir Gilbert at length. "You don't mean *that*. Why, he has one foot in the grave—a very old man—I was dining with him only a fortnight ago."

"Ah! Well, I think you are content now, Sir Gilbert?"

"It is terrible—terrible! I have the picture back, but I wouldn't have the scandal known for worlds."

"It never need be," replied Hazell. "You will make it all right with the Winchester people?"

"Yes—yes—even if I have to admit I was mistaken, and let the forgery stay through the exhibition."

"I think that would be the best way," replied Hazell, who never regretted his action.

"Of course, Jeffreys ought to have been punished," he said to himself; "but it was a clever idea—a clever idea!"

"May I offer you some lunch?" asked Sir Gilbert.

Thank you; but I am a vegetarian, and——"

"I think my cook could arrange something—let me ring."

"It is very good of you, but I ordered a dish of lentils and a salad at the station restaurant. But if you will allow me just to go through my physical training *ante* luncheon exercises here, it would save me the trouble of a more or less public display at the station."

"Certainly," replied the rather bewildered Baronet; whereupon Hazell threw off his coat and commenced whirling his arms like a windmill.

"Digestion should be considered *before* a meal," he explained.

V

HOW THE BANK WAS SAVED

THORPE HAZELL always looked upon the affair of
the Birmingham Bank from a distinctly humorous
point of view, declaring that it was really not worth
calling a railway mystery or adventure, and that it
scarcely called forth any astuteness on his part.
And yet there were facts in the case that are, perhaps,
worth recording.

The banking firm of Crosbie, Penfold, & Co. was
an old-established one in Birmingham, numbering
many of the leading manufacturers among its
customers. At the time of this story the firm
suddenly became aware that they had an enemy,
and that this enemy was no other than an exceedingly powerful multi-millionaire of Germanic Jewish
origin, named Peter Kinch. His reputation was
none of the best in the financial world, and it was
rumoured that he would stop at nothing to attain
an object.

He had a personal quarrel with the senior partner
of the bank—old Mr. Crosbie. Kinch's son had
met the latter's daughter abroad, and proposed to
her before the girl was old enough to know her own
mind. Her father was furious when he heard about
it, for the young man bore about the same reputation as his father ; and although there were hundreds

who looked upon him as a "good catch," old
Crosbie came of a Puritan family, and retained its
instincts strongly.

Samuel Kinch, who was only unbusinesslike
when matters concerned his son, whom he foolishly
idolised, went to see Mr. Crosbie on the matter,
and, it is said, offered to settle half-a-million on his
daughter if the old gentleman would consent to the
marriage.   This only made him more angry than
ever, and he retorted that the girl was not to be
sold.

A couple of years had passed since then, and
Phyllis Crosbie had forgotten her girlish love, and
was engaged to Charlie Penfold, the son of the
junior partner—the "Co.," in reality of the firm.
But Samuel Kinch had *not* forgotten.   Deep down
in that keen, financial brain of his was a strong
instinct of revenge for injuries, and he had taken
the affair as a personal slight.

However, outwardly he seemed to have made it
up.   He was occasionally in Birmingham on business and in contact with Mr. Crosbie, and he never
referred to the subject.   Then, one day, he deposited
the sum of two hundred thousand pounds with the
bank.

"I have so much business in Birmingham," he
explained, "that it will be a matter of great convenience if you will hold this money."

Old Crosbie didn't half like it, and proposed
keeping it intact in their strong room; but the
other partners prevailed upon him to invest it in
securities.   For some months nothing was heard
about it.   Then some strange rumours suddenly
got about with regard to the bank.   People began
to ask for their cash, and quite a little "run" was

taking place. Suddenly Peter Kinch announced that he wanted his two hundred thousand pounds immediately.

The partners were met in consultation in their private room at the bank, which was not yet opened to the public.

"Yes," said Mr. Crosbie, "he wants every penny of it to-morrow. We must face it."

"Under ordinary circumstances we could have paid easily," said Mr. Penfold senior, "but it's very awkward just now. I can't understand matters."

"I can," said old Mr. Crosbie; "I believe we're the victims of a plot, and that Kinch is working it."

"But his object?" asked Charles Penfold.

"Partly private, perhaps—but there's something else at the bottom of it, and he could well afford to sacrifice his money here altogether if he gained his ends."

"What is it?" asked Charles and his father simultaneously.

"Railway contracts," replied Mr. Crosbie. "It's a question of cutting German estimates by Hill & Co. and a couple of other firms here. If we were to stop payment there would be a serious lack of ready money, because those three firms do most of their business with us. If they can't be sure of ready money now, they daren't undertake the contracts at the price they could otherwise have done. And in steps the German firm, and the firm in question, gentlemen, is really Samuel Kinch. It's a smart bit of business."

He rose from his seat and took a glance out of the window.

"Look here," he said to the others.

It was ten minutes to ten, the hour when the

bank opened, and already five or six people were waiting outside, one of them with a cheque fluttering in his hand, tapping the pavement impatiently with his stick. It was obvious that trouble was ahead.

" H'm," exclaimed Mr. Penfold. " I suppose we can hold out to-day."

" Yes, for to-day," replied the senior partner grimly. " We have a fair supply of cash, and I don't think there's any danger. But we must have some more before we open to-morrow. We had better ask Simpson to bring us the securities at once. Also we will telegraph to the Imperial and City, asking them to get the money ready for us. Then, perhaps you, Mr. Charles, and Simpson could go up by the 11.12 train and bring it down this evening ? "

The Imperial and City Bank acted as London agents for Crosbie, Penfold, & Co., and it would be their office to raise the necessary funds on the firm's securities. A busy hour was passed in going over these documents and signing transfers. Meanwhile, a steady stream of customers kept coming into the bank, and the cashiers were hard at work paying out money.

Simpson, one of the senior cashiers, who had been selected to accompany Charles Penfold to London, was a particularly smart and level-headed fellow.

" I should like to tell you of a rumour I heard last night, sir," he said to Mr. Crosbie, when the securities had been looked over and packed in a strong leather bag.

" Yes—what is it ? "

" Well, sir, we have a powerful enemy, and not over scrupulous . . . am I right, sir ? "

" Quite right.   What of that ? "

" It would be to his interest to prevent us from getting this money in time, sir, and he might not be particular as to what means he took to do it.   One of the juniors was asked a lot of questions about us last night by a suspicious-looking stranger he met— er—well, in a bar.   He didn't let out anything, but he told me about it, and just now he saw this same man hanging about the bank.

"Thank you," said Mr. Penfold.   " Of course, Charles," he went on, "you will take every precaution. You had better telegraph to Scotland Yard, and ask for a detective to travel back with you this evening."

" I'll do better than that, father.   I'll wire to my friend Thorpe Hazell.   What he doesn't know about railways isn't worth knowing, and I'll ask him to meet me at the Imperial and City.   He'll probably come back with us, and I'd really rather have him than an ordinary detective.   If there's going to be any attempt at robbery on the line, his advice will be the best to act upon, I'm sure."

Thus it came to pass that Thorpe Hazell found himself in consultation with Charles Penfold a little after three o'clock that day in a private room at the Imperial and City Bank, which, as everyone knows, is situated in Throgmorton Street.

" I'm sure we are being carefully watched," said Penfold.   " You noticed it, didn't you, Simpson ? "

" Distinctly, sir.   Not only on the train, but I'm certain a taxi followed us here." '

" Well," replied Hazell, "the thing is very obvious.   You say you have reason to believe that an attempt is going to be made to rob you of this large sum of money.   By the way, what does it consist of and how do you propose to carry it ? "

" Mostly of Bank of England notes, but a certain amount of gold. We shall pack it in this bag. If we all three travel with it, it ought to be safe."

" Well, I'm not so sure of that," said Hazell; " from what you tell me, we evidently have a very wily enemy to deal with, and my experience of railway mysteries tells me there is not always safety in numbers. What train did you think of taking ? "

" The 4.55 from Paddington. But if you advised it we might travel by another route."

" Quite so. But the enemy might have thought of that, too, and taken steps accordingly. We must be prepared for all emergencies. Now, suppose you tell me exactly why you think this attempt is likely to be made. Is there any ulterior motive besides robbery ? "

Penfold explained that there was, telling Hazell the question of the German contracts. The latter's face brightened during the recital.

" Tell me," he said, " suppose your hypothesis is correct and the robbery took place, what would happen ? "

" Well, Kinch would know at once, I expect, and would wire to Germany without delay, anticipating the fact that we should have to stop payment to-morrow. He has everything ready, we know."

" Ah, and suppose he wired and put the machinery in motion, and after all you *could* pay to-morrow, what about that ? "

" He wouldn't be such a fool. Why, it would cost him a million. Sure to. Perhaps more. When a man like Kinch once makes a slip it's pretty bad for his reputation."

Hazell got up from his chair and slapped Penfold on the shoulder.

"Excellent, my dear chap," he exclaimed; "I thought at first you were only bringing me an ordinary case of prevention of robbery in a train. But this is really likely to be interesting. Quite a little comedy, in fact. That is, if you will place yourself in my hands entirely ? "

"Very well," replied Penfold, "but I don't quite see your meaning."

"Ah, you're rather tired and run down, you see. This affair is making you over anxious. Let me recommend a few hours at the seaside. Bournemouth, now, is a capital place. And, by the way, Mr. Simpson," he went on, addressing the cashier, "it's close on half-past three. Not too soon in the afternoon for a cup of tea. There's an A. B. C. fifty yards from the bank. Go and get some tea, my dear sir, and come back in a quarter of an hour's time; and would you mind bringing me a pint of milk in a bottle and a packet of plasmon chocolate? I shall have to dine *en route*."

Penfold stared at him in amazement, but Hazell insisted. As soon as he was out of the room Hazell exclaimed :

"Quick now—see the directors here and get the cash; it ought to be ready now. Have it as much in notes as possible. We must pack that bag before Simpson returns. I'm afraid I'm going to impose on him a little. Ah, and I shall want another bag —mine will do. I brought it with me in case I was out for the night; and we'll ask the people here to lend us some weights, or anything heavy will do."

He emptied the things out of his bag, two of the directors came in with the money a few minutes afterwards, and then Penfold began to see daylight. Meanwhile Hazell was rapidly turning over the leaves of a Bradshaw and jotting down notes on a bit of paper, which he presently handed to Penfold.

"Follow these directions carefully. It's best for you to keep out of the way. Now then, here comes Simpson. Not a word, gentlemen, please!"

"Well, Mr. Simpson," he went on, as the cashier came in, "Mr. Penfold agrees with me that you had better take the money down with me. He's not feeling very well, and he's going for a little holiday. You will have to explain matters to his partners. You and I will start directly, but I'm going to see Mr. Penfold off first. Come along, old fellow, you'll catch the 4.10 to Bournemouth easily."

He took him outside the bank, holding his bag in his hand, hailed a hansom, and, as Penfold got in, said to him in a loud tone of voice:

"Don't you worry, old chap. I'll see this thing through. It's much better for you to keep out of it, because Simpson and I can manage it. I hope you'll find your sister better when you get to Bournemouth; it may not be so bad as the telegram makes out."

He noticed, to his intense delight, that a man who was lounging past dropped his stick on the pavement close by, and stopped to pick it up.

"Good-bye, Penfold—oh, I was nearly forgetting your bag; here you are. "Now then, my man," he added, addressing the chauffeur, "Waterloo Station, sharp!"

He had the satisfaction of seeing the man who had dropped the stick hail another hansom, which followed in the wake of Penfold's.

"Ah," he said, "they'll see he takes a ticket for Bournemouth, and they won't suspect anything. Now for a little adventure!"

A quarter of an hour later he was seated in a taxi-cab with Simpson, *en route* for Paddington. The leather bag, heavy with the weight of its contents, lay on the floor in front of them. Once or twice Hazell put his head out of the window and looked behind, laughing softly to himself when he drew it back.

"Now, Mr. Simpson," he said to his companion, presently, "you and I are about to run the gauntlet. Perhaps you may think my conduct a little strange, later, but I must beg of you not to question it."

"Very well," replied Simpson, who had hardly taken his eyes off the precious bag in front of him, " I have every confidence in you, Mr. Hazell."

" That's right. Now, suppose—mind, I only say *suppose*—you and I are attacked on the train to-night, you would defend that bag of money, eh ? "

Simpson turned to him in surprise.

" Of course——" he began, but a smile on the other's face stopped him.

" It is a considerable sum, I know," he said, " but not so valuable as a human life—*if* you were threatened, Mr. Simpson, eh ? "

Again the smile crept over his face, and puzzled the cashier for a moment.

" *I* should prefer to save my life, I think," went on Hazell. " Let us look at the matter seriously. You are attacked, we'll say, and the odds are too great. The villains get away with the money. Perhaps you are able to stop the train. But the money has disappeared. You would go to Mr. Crosbie when you reached Birmingham, and tell him of this terrible misfortune. You would tell the police. This fellow, Kinch, if he's at the bottom of it, would. put his little plan in action at once. Dear me! A most 'regrettable incident,' as politicians call it. You would throw the whole blame on me. And then—and then—let us suppose that after all the money was at the bank the next morning. What a surprise! Villainy defeated—virtue triumphant. No! Don't ask me any questions. Here we are at Paddington."

A broad grin broke out on Simpson's face as he got out.

"Be careful of the precious bag," said Hazell. "That's right."

The short winter's day was drawing to a close, and darkness had begun to set in. Hazell looked, suspiciously, all round him, and kept close to Simpson, helping him to carry the heavy bag. They took first-class tickets for Birmingham, and tipped the guard to secure them a compartment. On Hazell giving Simpson directions, the latter got in with the bag, and Hazell stood outside on the platform as if on guard.

Presently an old clergyman came along with shuffling step. He was about to get into the same compartment, when Hazell stopped him, telling him it was engaged. He bowed politely, and got into the next one. The carriage was well up the platform and in front of the train, and the majority of the passengers were getting in behind, as is often the case at terminal stations.

A few minutes before the train started a couple of men—strong-looking fellows—came marching up the platform and got into the compartment immediately in front of Simpson. They were dressed rather like farmers, and one of them carried a heavy stick

The positions of the travellers in this particular carriage were now as follows :

1st compartment—the two men.

2nd   „   —Simpson.

3rd   „   —the old clergyman.

Hazell still stood outside the door on the platform. The hand of the great clock was almost on the moment of departure when he suddenly exclaimed :

" I've forgotten to get a paper.   There's just time."

He ran back to the bookstall.   At the same moment the old clergyman put his head out of the window and watched him.   He bought his paper and started back.

At that exact moment the guard waved his green lamp, the whistle sounded, and the train began very slowly to move.

" Look sharp, sir ! "

Then Hazell did a very clumsy thing.   He caught his toe in the platform and fell, sprawling.

The next moment he was on his feet, but it was too late to catch his compartment.   He made a rush for the next carriage; his keen eyes detected an empty compartment ; he opened the door and swung himself into the moving train.   Simpson, who had his head out of the window, saw what had happened.   At first he felt strangely disconcerted, and then, once more, he broke into a smile.

The first stop was at Oxford.   Hazell lit a cigar and threw himself back in his seat, laughing softly to himself.

" They are really a very clumsy lot," he soliloquised, " my reputation is quite at stake in allowing it.   Never mind, though."

From time to time he looked out of the window towards the front of the train, but it was not until they had travelled a considerable distance beyond Reading that the comedy he was expecting began to be played.

Then he saw, in the darkness, the door of the compartment in front of Simpson's open, and a figure on the footboard. Darting to the other side and looking out of that window he could just discern someone on that side of the carriage also.

Simpson was sitting in his compartment, wondering what was going to happen. Suddenly there was an awful crashing of glass, and the window on the left-hand side was splintered to bits by a violent blow from a stick from outside. Involuntarily Simpson first started back, and then sprang at the window.

The ruse succeeded admirably, for at the same moment the opposite door was opened and a man sprang in. Before Simpson knew what had happened, he felt himself seized by the collar from behind and dragged back. Then the door with the splintered window opened, and the second villain threw himself upon him. Resistance was out of the question. In three minutes Simpson lay on the seat, his hands and feet tied, and a handkerchief bound over his mouth.

"There," said one of the men, "that little job's done. It's lucky for you my friend, that that clumsy detective isn't in with you, or we might have had to use *this*," and he showed a revolver. "But we shan't hurt you. We're just going to search you to see if you have any notes on you, in case they're not all in the bag."

They set to work, coolly enough, but found nothing.

"Well," went on the man, "now we'll clear out. Sorry to have troubled you," he added, to the cashier, "but you should have taken more care of your property. By George, it's precious heavy!"

"Ready?" asked the other.

"Yes—where are we?"

"Between Cholsey and Didcot."

"Right!"

He gave a sharp tug at the chain of the communication-cord with which every Great Western express is provided inside the carriages. A moment or two later there was a shrieking of the engine whistle and a grinding of the brakes.

As the train slowed down the two men, taking the heavy bag with them, prepared to get out. The one who held the bag was actually on the footboard before the train stopped, and Hazell, who was watching from his window, distinctly saw what happened.

The train came to a standstill on an embankment, and the two robbers jumped and ran for all they were worth, but not before more than one of the passengers had caught a glimpse of them. The guard came running along the train, together with Hazell.

The latter made for Simpson's compartment, and was taken a little aback when he found him lying prostrate, but a couple of seconds sufficed to show he was unhurt. He tore the gag off, and the two of them raised a hue-and-cry that was heard all along the train.

"What is it?" asked the guard.

"Robbery!" shouted Simpson, as they cut his bonds, "thousands of pounds, man."

"Money for a Birmingham bank," explained Hazell. "I was in charge of it with the cashier here, only I nearly got left behind at Paddington and travelled in another compartment. Quick! They mustn't escape!"

"What was the money in?" asked the guard, who thought the men a couple of fools to travel with it as they had done.

"A leather bag—they must have taken it off—there were two of them."

"I saw them running down the embankment," exclaimed a passenger who had joined them, "but I'll swear they were carrying nothing. They vaulted over the fence at the bottom, and each of them used both his hands."

Hazell was standing beside the train and a frown swept over his face. He glanced up quickly at the elderly clergyman, who was looking out of the window.

"Did you see them, sir?" he asked.

"Yes—yes."

"Could you make out if they carried a bag?"

"Oh, yes—I'm sure they did."

"And I'll swear they didn't," said the dogged passenger.

"We'll search the train—sharp, please," said the guard, and he mounted into the old clergyman's compartment at once. But there was nothing there. Nor could anything be discovered in or near the train.

"Now," said the guard, "I'm very sorry gentlemen, but I can't delay the train longer. You should have carried the money in my van. All I can do is to stop at Didcot to let you get out and send a telegram or see the police. That's your affair. It's evident they've made off. Take your seats, please ! "

One or two passengers who had started on a chase on the spur of the moment came panting back. Hazell nudged Simpson, and they climbed up into the compartment occupied by the clergyman.

" This is not your carriage," he said mildly, as the train started.

" Oh—so I see," said Hazell. " Never mind. This is a terrible thing—terrible ! " and he went on to discuss the robbery.

" You had better wire from Didcot to Mr. Crosbie," he said to Simpson, " see the police there, and then come on to Birmingham by a later train."

" What shall you do ? "

" Oh, I think I'll go on. Of course you'll also wire back to London to have the notes stopped. That's all we can do, I think."

An almost imperceptible smile passed over the face of the old clergyman.

" Was it all in notes, may I ask ? "

" Oh, no. There was a considerable sum in gold," replied Hazell, who, even for an amateur detective, was strangely communicative.

At Oxford the old clergyman got out for a moment. Hazell saw him hand a paper to an official, and the latter made for the telegraph office. When he came back to the carriage he got into another compartment. Hazell followed him, a sweet smile on his face. The old clergyman grew very grumpy and uneasy.

But Hazell stuck to him like a leech—not only to Birmingham, but all the way to Chester. The old gentleman became more and more uneasy as the train went on. He even told Hazell that he wished to be

alone. But Hazell only smiled, and offered excuses.
Then he introduced the subject of physical culture,
explaining the desirability of lentil and plasmon diet,
and giving practical explanation of "nerve training" by holding a piece of paper in front of his face
at arm's length and keeping the edge in line with
the hat-rack opposite. When they got to Chester
he stood about on the platform till the empty train
was backed off into a siding.

Then the old gentleman, who had been hovering
about the train also, lost his temper, and swore
under his breath.

*   *   *   *   *   *

Old Mr. Crosbie and Mr. Penfold, senior, sat in
their private room in the bank, with Simpson standing before them. The latter was having a very bad
time of it indeed. Questions and rebukes were
being hurled at his devoted head by the two
partners.

"I cannot understand it at all, can you, Penfold?"

"No," said the latter, "and I'm bound to say I
think you have acted in a very strange manner,
Simpson. You may go to your place—but there is
a detective in the bank, and he has orders to see
that you don't leave."

All the papers were full of the robbery that morning. A little crowd had gathered outside the bank
waiting for the doors to open. Several Birmingham
firms were in consternation. The partners, who
had been up all night, looked at each other blankly.

"Can we open?" asked Mr. Crosbie in a hoarse
whisper.

The other shook his head.

"We daren't," he groaned.

A few minutes passed in silence. The clock in the office marked seven minutes to the hour. A cab dashed up outside.

The next moment Charles Penfold, fresh and smiling, stood before the partners, opening a bag, and turning out his pockets before their astounded gaze. There was no time for explanation.

Five minutes later the doors of the bank opened, and the foremost of the crowd outside entered, wondering what was about to happen. By common consent they gave way to a coarse-looking man who was forcing his way to the paying-out counter, a smile of triumph on his evil features. For they recognised him as the Nemesis of the bank, Samuel Kinch himself, who had come to take his revenge in person.

He slammed down a cheque upon the counter. The cashier turned it over carelessly to see the indorsement. He did not even ask him to step into the partners' room. He had his instructions.

"You will take it in notes, I suppose, sir?" he asked coolly.

"Yes, if you've got enough," replied Kinch insolently.

"Oh, that's all right, sir."

There was a dead silence, broken only by the rustle and crackling of roll after roll of Bank of England notes as the cashier counted them out and Kinch checked them, with a snarling expression on his face.

Then arose a hum and a buzz. Kinch had been paid. For half-an-hour the paying cashiers were fairly busy, but the tide was beginning to turn, and in an hour's time the receiving cashiers were doing all the work.

The credit of Crosbie, Penfold & Co. was saved, and the tenders for the railway contracts could be delivered without fear of lack of cash for preliminary expenses and raw material.

" One in the eye for old Kinch ! " was the verdict of the day.

* * * * * *

" Oh, the thing was childish ! " said Hazell that evening at the snug little dinner to which old Mr. Crosbie had invited him, but at which he only ate his " plasmon," and partook of seven raw apples—the other partner, Charles Penfold, and Simpson were also present—" I saw that if there was a sham robbery this cunning Samuel Kinch would heap vengeance on himself. So I sent Mr. Charles Penfold here down to Bournemouth, his pockets stuffed with notes, and my own bag stuffed with gold, and slung on the roof of a hansom to avoid suspicion. It would be difficult for them to connect Bournemouth with Birmingham, but we managed to do so by a devious route.

" Then I filled the leather bag with weights and things. Simpson, *of course*, thought we had the money, ha ! ha ! ha ! Oh, *don't* say you didn't, Simpson —don't spoil it. It was a clumsy method of attack, but it answered."

" But what became of that bag ? "

" That's just the greatest joke of the whole thing. I was looking out of the window, Simpson, as the beggars got off, and I saw them hand the bag to that sweet old clergyman. The train had hardly stopped before he was out of it. He climbed to the roof of the carriage by the steps at the end, put the bag on the top, and was in at the other side of his compartment in a jiffy. I travelled all the way to Chester to prevent him from laying his hands on that bag, and he was furious. It may be going about the country in that fashion still, for all we know."

" But why prevent him when it was of no value ?." asked Mr. Crosbie.

" That was just it. If he had once discovered it was only a sham robbery he would have given the alarm to Kinch—and that would have spoilt all."

" Well, Mr. Hazell. I'm sure the Bank is deeply indebted to you."

" Not at all. It has been a very ludicrous little adventure, and I've thoroughly enjoyed it."

Here he suddenly jumped from his seat, threw himself on his back on the floor, stretching his arms over his head as far as they could reach.

" Good gracious," exclaimed old Mr. Crosbie, "what's the matter ? Are you ill ? "

" I should be," replied Hazell gravely, "very probably, if I did not take fifty deep breaths in a recumbent position. It is the secret of digesting fruit ! "

VI

THE AFFAIR OF THE GERMAN
DISPATCH-BOX

THORPE HAZELL often said afterwards that the most daring case which he ever undertook was that of the German Dispatch-Box. It was an affair of international importance at the time, and, for obvious reasons, remained shrouded in mystery. Now, however, when it may be relegated to the region of obsolete diplomatic crises, there is no reason why it should not, to a certain extent, be made public.

Hazell was only half through his breakfast one morning at his house in Netherton, when a telegram arrived for him with this message :

Am coming by next train. Wish to consult you on important question.

MOSTYN COTTERELL.

"Cotterell, Cotterell," said Hazell to himself. "Oh, yes, I remember—he was on the same staircase with myself at St. Philip's. A reading man in those days. I haven't seen him for years. Surely he's something in the Government now. Let me see."

He got his Whitaker and consulted its pages. Presently he found what he wanted.

"Under-Secretary for Foreign Affairs—Mostyn Cotterell."

As soon as he had finished his breakfast, including his pint of lemonade, he produced a "Book of Exercises," and carefully went through the following directions:

"Stand in correct position, commence to inhale, and at the same time commence to tense the muscles of the arms, and raise them to an extended front horizontal position; leave the hands to drop limp from the wrists. While doing this change the weight of the body from the full foot on to the toes; in this position hold the breath and make rigid and extended the muscles of the arms, sides, neck, abdomen, and legs. Repeat this fifteen times."

Half-an-hour or so later Mostyn Cotterell was ushered into his room. He was a tall, thin man, with a black moustache that made his naturally pale face look almost white. There was a haggard look about him, and certain dark lines under his eyes showed pretty plainly that he was suffering from want of sleep.

"It's a good many years since we met, Hazell," he began, "and you have gained quite a reputation since the old college days."

"Ah, I see you have read my monograph on 'Nerve Culture and Rational Food,'" replied Hazell.

"Never heard of it," said Cotterell. "No, I mean your reputation as a railway expert, my dear fellow."

"Oh, railways!" exclaimed Hazell in a disappointed tone of voice. "They're just a hobby of mine, that's all. Is that why you've come?"

"Exactly. I called at your flat in town, but was

told you were here. I want to consult you on a delicate matter, Hazell; one in which your knowledge of-railways may prove of great value. Of course, it is understood that what I am going to say is quite private."

"Certainly."

"Well, let me put a case. Suppose a man was travelling, say, from London to the Continent by the ordinary boat train; and suppose that it was desirable to prevent that man from getting to his destination, would it—well—would it be possible to prevent him doing so?"

Hazell smiled.

"Your enigma is a difficult one to answer," he said. "It would all depend upon the means you cared to employ. I daresay it could be done, but you would probably have to resort to force."

"That would hardly be politic. I want you to suggest some plan by which he could be got into a wrong train, or got out of the right one, so that, let us say, something he was carrying would be lost, or, at least, delayed in transit."

"You are not very clear, Cotterell. First you speak of the *man* being frustrated, and then of something he is carrying. What do you mean? Which is of the greater importance—the man or his property?"

"His property."

"That puts a different aspect on it. I take it this is some intrigue of your profession. Why not place confidence in me, and tell me the whole thing? I never like to work on supposition. Once some fellows tried to draw me on a supposed case of wrecking a train. I could have told them half-a-dozen theories of my own invention, but I held my tongue, and lucky it was that I did so, for I found out afterwards they belonged to an American train robber gang. I don't accuse you of any nefarious purposes, but if you want my advice, tell me the exact circumstances. Only, I warn you beforehand, Cotterell, that I won't give you any tips that would either compromise me or be of danger to any railway company."

"Very well," replied the Under-Secretary, "I will tell you the leading facts without betraying any State secrets, except to mention that there is a great stake involved. To cut matters short, a very important document has been stolen from our office. We pretty well know the culprit, only we have no proof. But we are certain of one thing and that is that this document is at present in the hands of the German Ambassador. You will understand that the ways of diplomacy are very subtle and that it is a case which makes action very difficult. If we were to demand the surrender of this paper we should be met, I have no doubt, with a bland denial that it is in the Ambassador's possession.

"Of course we have our secret agents, and they have told us that Colonel Von Kriegen, one of the messengers of the German Embassy, has been ordered to start at mid-day with dispatches to Berlin. It is more than likely—in fact it is a dead certainty—that this particular document will be included in his dispatches. Now, if it once gets into the possession of the German Chancellery, there will be a bad international trouble which might even land us in a Continental war. If you can devise any means of obstructing or preventing the transit of this dispatch you would be rendering the country a real service."

Hazell thought for a moment.

" Do you think this Colonel Von Kriegen knows of the document he is carrying ? " he asked presently.

" I shouldn't think so, its contents are of far too much importance to trust even to a regular messenger. No, he will probably be told to exercise the greatest care, and his journey will be watched and himself guarded by the German secret police."

" How is he likely to carry the document ? "

" In his dispatch-box, together with other papers."

" And he will probably travel with secret police. My dear fellow, you have given me a hard nut to crack. Let me think a bit."

He lit a cigarette and smoked hard for a few minutes. Presently he asked Cotterell if the dispatch-box had a handle to it.

" Yes—of course," replied the Under-Secretary; "a leather handle."

" I wish I knew exactly what it was like."

" I can easily tell you. All the dispatch-boxes of the German Embassy are of the same pattern. It is our business to know the smallest details. It would be about a foot long, eight inches broad, and about five inches deep, with a handle on the top—a dark green box."

Hazell's face lit up with sudden interest.

" You haven't one exactly like it ? " he asked.

" Yes, we have. At my office."

" Will the key be with the Colonel ? "

" Of course not. The Ambassador here will lock it, and it will not be opened till it is in the hands of the Chancellor in Berlin."

Hazell jumped to his feet and began to stride up and down the room.

" Cotterell ! " he exclaimed, " there's just one plan that occurs to me. It's a very desperate one, and even if it succeeds it will land me in prison."

" In England ? " asked the other.

" Rather. I'm not going to play any tricks on the Continent, I can tell you. Now, suppose I'm able to carry out this plan and am imprisoned—say at Dovehaven—what would happen ? "

He stopped abruptly in his walk and looked at Cotterell. A grin broke over the latter's face, and he said, quietly :

" Oh—you'd escape, Hazell."

" Very good. I shall want help. *You'd* better not come. Have you got a knowing fellow whom you can trust ? He must be a sharp chap, mind."

" Yes, I have. One of our private men, named Bartlett."

" Good. There are just two hours before the Continental train starts, and a quarter of an hour before you get a train back to town. You wire Bartlett from Netherton to meet you, and I'll write out instructions for you to give him. He'll have an hour in which to carry them out."

He wrote rapidly for five minutes upon a sheet of paper, and then handed it over to the Under-Secretary.

" Mind you," he said, " the chances are terribly against us, and I can only promise to do my best. I shall follow you to town by another train that will give me just time to catch the boat express. What is this Von Kriegen like ? "

Cotterell described him.

" Good—now you must be off ! "

Three-quarters of an hour later Hazell came out of his house, somewhat changed in appearance. He had put on the same dark wig which he wore in the affair of Crane's cigars, and was dressed in a black serge suit and straw hat. A clerical collar completed the deception of a clergyman in semi-mufti.

*   *   *   *   *   *

A stiffly-upright, military-looking man, with the ends of his fair moustache strongly waxed, dressed in a frock coat suit and tall hat, and carrying a dispatch-box, walked down the platform beside the boat train, the guard, who knew him well by sight—as he knew many who travelled on that line with their precious dispatches—giving him a salute as he passed.

Two men walked closely, but unobtrusively behind the Colonel; two men whose eyes and ears were on the alert, and who scrutinised everyone carefully as they passed along. Of their presence the Special Messenger took not the slightest notice, though he was well aware of their companionship. He selected a first-class compartment, and got in. The two men followed him into the carriage, but without saying a word. One of them posted himself by the window, and kept a steady look out on to the platform.

The train was just about to start, and the guard had just put his whistle to his mouth, when a man came running down the platform, a small bag in one hand, a bundle of papers and an umbrella in the other. It was only a clergyman, and the man at the window gave a smile as he saw him.

With a rush, the clergyman made for the compartment, seizing the handle of the door and opening it. Frantically he threw his bag, umbrella, and papers into the carriage. The train had just begun to move.

The man near the window had retreated at the

onslaught. He was just about to resent the intrusion with the words that the compartment was engaged, when a porter, running up behind the clergyman, pushed him in and slammed the door.

"I thought I'd lost it!" exclaimed the intruder, taking off his hat and wiping the perspiration from his forehead, for it was a very hot day, and he had been hurrying. "It was a close shave! Oh, thank you, thank you!" he added, as one of the men rather ungraciously picked up his bag and papers from the floor, at the same time eyeing him closely.

But Hazell, in his disguise, was perfectly proof against any suspicion. He sat down and opened the *Guardian* with an easy air, just looking round at each of his three companions in such a naturally inquisitive manner as to thoroughly disarm them from the outset. The Colonel had lighted a cigar and said, half apologetically, as he took it from his lips:

"I hope you don't mind smoking?"

"Oh, not at all. I do it myself occasionally," returned the clergyman with an amiable smile.

The train was now fairly under way, and Hazell was beginning, as he read his paper, to take mental stock of his surroundings and the positions in which the other three were seated.

He, himself, was facing the engine on the left-hand side of the compartment, close to the window. Immediately opposite to him sat Colonel von Kriegen, watchful and alert, although he seemed to smoke so complacently. Beside the Colonel, on the seat on his left, was the precious dispatch-box; and the Colonel's hand, as it dangled negligently over the arm-rest, touched it ever and anon. On the next seat, guarding the dispatch-box on that side, sat one of the secret police agents, while the other had placed himself next to Hazell and, consequently, opposite the box, which was thus thoroughly guarded at all points.

It was this dispatch-box that Hazell was studying as he apparently read his paper, noting its exact position and distance from him. As he had told Morton Cotterell, the chances of carrying out his plan were very much against him, and he felt that this was) more than ever the case now. He had really hoped to secure a seat beside the box. But this was out of the question.

After a bit he put down his paper, leant forward, and looked out of the window, watching the country as they sped through it. Once, just as they were passing through a station, he stood up and leant his head out of the window for a minute. The three men exchanged glances now that his back was turned, but the Colonel only smiled and shook his head slightly.

Then Hazell sat down once more, yawned, gathered up his paper, and made another apparent attempt to read it. After a bit, he drew a cigarette case from his pocket, took out a cigarette, and placed it in his mouth. Then he leant forward, in a very natural attitude, and began feeling in his waistcoat pocket for a match.

The German Colonel watched him, carelessly flicking the ash from his cigar as he did so. Then, as it was apparent that the clergyman could find no matches, his politeness came to the front.

"You want a light, sir," he said in very good English, "can I offer you one?"

"Oh, thanks!" replied Hazell, shifting to the

edge of his seat, and leaning still more forward, "perhaps I may take one from your cigar ? "

Every action that followed had been most carefully thought out beforehand. As he leant over towards the German he turned his back slightly on the man who sat beside him. He held the cigarette with the first and second fingers of his right hand and with the end of it in his mouth. He kept his eyes fixed on the Colonel's. Meanwhile his left hand went out through the open window, dropped over the sill, remained there a moment, then came back, and crossed over the front of his body stealthily with the palm downwards.

It was all over in a second, before either of the three had time to grasp what was happening. He had his face close up to the Colonel's, and had taken a puff at the cigarette, when suddenly his left hand swooped down on the handle of the dispatch-box, his right hand flew forward into the Colonel's face, instantly coming round with a quick sweep to his left hand, and, before the Colonel could recover or either of the others take action, he had tossed the dispatch-box out of the window.

They were on him at once. He sprang up, back to the window, and made a little struggle, but the Colonel and one of the others had him on the seat in no time. Meanwhile the third man had pulled the electric safety signal, and had dashed to the window. Thrusting his head out, he looked back along the level bit of line on which they were running.

"I can see it!" he cried triumphantly, as his eye caught a dark object beside the track. The whole affair had taken place so suddenly that the train began to pull up within fifteen or twenty seconds of the throwing out of the dispatch case. There was a shrill whistle, a grinding of brakes, and the train came to a standstill.

The guard was out of his van in an instant, running along beside the train.

"What is it?" he asked, as he came up to the carriage.

The police agent, who still kept his eyes fixed back on the track, beckoned him to come up. Heads were out of windows, and this matter was a private one. So the guard climbed on to the footboard.

"A dispatch-box has been thrown out of the carriage," whispered the police agent; "we have the man here. But we *must* get the case. It's only a little way back. We pulled the signal at once—in fact, I could see it lying beside the track before we stopped."

"Very good, sir," replied the guard quietly, commencing to wave an arm towards the rear of the train. The signal was seen on the engine, and the train began to reverse. Very soon a small, dark object could be seen alongside the rails. As they drew close, the guard held out his hand motionless, the train stopped, and he jumped off.

"Is this it?" he asked, as he handed in the dispatch-box.

"Yes!" exclaimed the Colonel, "it's all right. Thank you, guard. Here's something for your trouble. We'll hand over the fellow to the police at Dovehaven. It was a clumsy trick."

Colonel Von Kriegen lit another cigar as the train went on, and looked at Hazell, who sat between the two police agents. There was a half smile on the Colonel's lips as he said:

"I'm afraid you did not quite succeed, sir! It was a sharp thing to do, but it didn't go quite far enough. You might have been sure that in broad daylight, and with the means of stopping the train, that it was impossible. Who put you on to this?"

"I accept the entire responsibility myself," replied Hazell—"failure and all. I have only one favour to ask you. Will you allow me to eat my lunch?"

"Oh, certainly," replied the Colonel grimly—"especially as you won't have a chance of doing so when we arrive at Dovehaven. I should like you to travel all the way with us, but the exigencies of international law prevent that."

Hazell bowed, and the next moment was placidly consuming Plasmon biscuits and drinking sterilised milk, expatiating at intervals on "natural food."

"Try a diet of macaroni and Dutch cheese," were his last words to the Colonel. "They both help to build up the grey brain material. Useful in your position!"

When the train arrived at Dovehaven, Hazell was given into the charge of the police there, and marched off to the station. Here the superintendent looked at him curiously. Hazell met his gaze, but nothing was said. It was strange, however, that he was not locked up in an ordinary cell, but in a small room.

It was also strange that the bar of the window was very loose, and that no one was about when he dropped out of it that night. The German police, when they heard about it, smiled. Diplomatic affairs are peculiar, and they knew that this particular "criminal" would never be caught.

Meanwhile, the Colonel journeyed on to Berlin, with the full assurance in his mind that the papers in his dispatch-box were intact. He duly handed the latter over in person to the Chancellor, who, as the result of a cypher telegram, was eagerly expecting it.

Somehow, his key did not fit the lock of the dispatch-box. After trying it for a few moments, he exclaimed :

"Colonel, how is this? This is not one of our boxes, surely?"

The Colonel's face turned pale, and he hesitated to reply. Snatching up a knife, the Chancellor forced open the box, a cry of dismay issuing from his lips as he drew out the contents—the current number of *Punch*, in which he figured in a cartoon, and a copy of the *Standard*, containing an article, carefully marked, on the foreign policy of the Government. Insult to injury, if you like.

German oaths never look well in print, and, anyhow, it is needless to record the ensuing conversation between the Chancellor and Colonel Von Kriegen. At about the time it was taking place the German Ambassador in London received by post the original dispatch-box and its contents, minus the incriminating document, which now reposed safely in the custody of the Foreign Office, thanks to the ingenuity of Thorpe Hazell.

*   *   *   *   *   *

"How was it done?" said Hazell afterwards, when telling the story to a companion. "Oh, it was a pure trick, and I hardly expected to be able to bring it off. Fortunately, Bartlett was a 'cute chap, and followed out all my instructions to the letter. Those instructions were very simple. I told him to wear an Inverness cloak, to provide himself with the duplicate dispatch-box, a few yards of very strong

fishing twine, a fair-sized snap-hook, and a light
walking-stick with a forked bit of wire stuck in the
end of it. The only difficulty about his job was the
presence of other travellers in his compartment,
but, as it happened, there were only two maiden
ladies, who thought him mad on fresh air.

"Of course, I told him how to use his various
articles, and also that on no account was he to
communicate with me either by word or look,
but that he was to get into the compartment next
to that in which the Colonel was travelling, and to
be ready to command either window by reserving a
seat with a bag on one side and seating himself on
the other.

"The cloak served for a double purpose—to hide
the dispatch-box and to conceal his movements from
the occupants of his carriage when the time for
action came. Fortunately, both his companions sat
with their backs to the engine, so that he was easily
able to command either window.

"I was to let him know which side of the train
was the sphere of action by putting out my head as
we ran through Eastwood. He would then look out
of both windows and get to work accordingly.

"What he did was this. He had the snap-hook
tied tightly to the end of the fishing-line. By leaning out of the window and slinging this hook on the
fork of his walking-stick he was able to reach it
along the side of the carriage—holding his stick at
the other end—and slip the hook over the handle
outside my door, where it hung by its cord.

"He then dropped the stick and held the cord
loosely in his right hand, the slack end ready to run
out. This, you will observe, kept the hook hanging
on my handle. With his left hand he drew the

dispatch-box from under his cloak and held it outside the carriage, ready to drop it instantly.

"Of course he was standing all the time, with his head and shoulders out of the window.

"When I leant forward to light my cigarette at the Colonel's cigar, I slipped my left hand out of the window, easily found the hook hanging there, grasped it, and kept it open with one finger. Bartlett, who was watching, got ready. You can easily guess the rest. I swung my left hand suddenly over to the dispatch-box, Bartlett allowing the line to run through his hand, snapped the hook over the handle before they could see what I was about, and pitched it out of the window as lightly as possible.

"The same instant Bartlett dropped the duplicate box from the train, grasped the line tightly as the real dispatch-box flew out, and hauled it in, hand over hand. He very soon had the dispatch-box safely stowed under his cloak, and, on reaching Dovehaven, took the next train back to town, to the no small satisfaction of his chief.

"Unluckily, I quite forgot to ask Cotterell to mention in the wire I knew he would be sending to the police at Dovehaven to have a dish of lentils ready for me in my brief imprisonment. It was very awkward. But they made me an exceedingly well-cooked tapioca pudding."

VII

HOW THE BISHOP KEPT HIS APPOINT-
MENT

"But," said the Bishop of Frattenbury, "while—er—agreeing with you on the question of consuming alcohol, I cannot follow what you say with regard to animal food. Many animals were—er—in point of fact designed by a beneficent Creator for the sustenance of human life."

"You've no small opinion of yourself, my lord," rejoined Thorpe Hazell, "if you really believe that the pig was created in order that *you* might have ham for breakfast."

The Bishop of Frattenbury reddened. He was not accustomed to be spoken to like this by a mere layman, and he would have resented it even in a church dignitary.

"I scarcely commend your flippant way of putting things, sir," he rejoined severely, "even for the sake of argument. I was alluding to the general scheme of creation, and the—er—fitness of things."

"But it amounts to this: You are in favour of killing pigs, and I am not," went on Hazell calmly, drawing a cigarette from his case; "and the question is: Are *you* a better Christian for killing your pigs, or am I, who have a certain amount of respect for the life of a hog, which you haven't?"

The Bishop frowned angrily.

"What you say is quite beside the mark," he answered; "I am not in the habit of taking the life of *any* animal."

"No; but you encourage butchery in others, which is degrading. But to go back to the subject we were discussing. Have you ever had any practical experience in the analysis of foodstuffs?"

"Of course not," said the Bishop; "I'm not a chemist."

"More's the pity, because, being a Bishop, it might be good for you to know something of the laws of health—capital subject for a charge to your clergy! Now, there are four excellent foods, each of them excelling the nutritive powers of animal flesh—oatmeal, macaroni, lentils, and Dutch cheese."

And he ticked them off one by one on his fingers.

"Really, sir!" exclaimed the Bishop, who was now in a very bad temper indeed, "I must ask you to excuse me from taking a further part in this conversation."

And, opening the book he had been reading, with a vicious gesture, he composed himself in the corner of the first-class compartment in which both were travelling. Thorpe Hazell smoked his cigarette quite calmly, a smile on his lips. He had not intended to say anything rude, but the Bishop's dogmatic manner had rather put his back up.

Presently he removed his coat, stood upright in the carriage, and commenced throwing his arms to and fro violently.

The Bishop of Frattenbury laid down his book and gazed at him in astonishment.

"A digestive exercise, my lord," explained Hazell, pausing for a moment. "It is now a quarter to seven, and I hope to dine at eight. You draw in a very deep breath—so!—then you move the arms ten times—so!—then you exhale the breath—slowly. It is also a safeguard against unnecessary flesh development. You should have practised it years ago!" And he lit a fresh cigarette.

There was a crash and a rattle and a heavy bumping. The Bishop was suddenly shot forward into Hazell's arms. The lamp went out, and total darkness followed. Then the carriage reeled like a drunken man, the panes of glass splintered, there was a dull shock, and Hazell, who had managed to get his hand outside the door and open it, fell out of the compartment on to the soft turf beside the line. He heard the Bishop follow him. A moment or two afterwards there was a heavy splash, and then a muffled cry somewhere below.

Thorpe Hazell blew the fragments of his cigarette out of his mouth, sat up, rubbed an injured elbow, and looked around him. There was an awful hissing of escaping steam from the engine. The driver was on the ground, a lamp in hand; another lamp was dancing about as the guard appeared on the scene.

"What's up?" cried Hazell, as he went towards the engine.

"She's off the line, sir," replied the man.

"Anyone hurt?" yelled the guard.

"I think not," replied the driver, "we weren't running fast. Jim!"

"Hullo!"

"All right?"

"Aye, mate, I jumped the other side," exclaimed the fireman.

"How about the passengers?" asked Hazell of the guard.

"There were only four in the train, sir," replied the guard—"two thirds—ah, here they are—yourself, and the Bishop."

"Ah, the Bishop, of course," said Hazell. "I think he got out just after me," he added, with a slight chuckle. "I hope he's not hurt."

At that moment a faint cry for help came from the foot of the embankment. Hazell and the guard hurried down, and there, by the light of the lamp, they beheld a sorry sight. At the bottom of the bank was a ditch, bordered by a barbed wire fence. The unfortunate prelate had fallen into the very muddiest part of the ditch, and in trying to emerge therefrom had caught his clothes on the barbed wire. He was a mass of mud from head to foot, his apron hung in ribbons, one of his coat tails was torn clean off, and one of his sleeves ripped up from elbow to wrist. Blood was trickling down his face from a slight cut on the cheek.

"Are you hurt, my lord?" asked Hazell.

"No," replied the Bishop grimly, "I don't think so—except a few bruises. But I'm exceedingly uncomfortable."

There was a look on the Bishop's muddy and bloodstained face as the lantern flashed upon him that suddenly appealed to Hazell.

He gave him his arm and helped him up the embankment. Then they found out what had happened to the little branch train in which they had been travelling. The crank axle of the tiny tank engine had broken, the leading wheels had left the rails, and one of the three carriages composing the train had jumped the metals with the shock. No one was hurt, and the Bishop's plight was really the worst of the lot.

The line upon which the catastrophe had taken place was the little branch one from Heston to Cathfield, a distance of some seven miles, and a single track.   Only four or five trains are timed to run per day upon this little bit of line, and even then it scarcely pays the company to run them, so small is the traffic.   This train, from Heston to Cathfield, was the last one of the day.   It was a winter's evening, exceedingly dark, and a hurried consultation took place between guard and passengers as to what was the best thing to be done.

"We're about three miles from Heston," said the former, "and it's impossible, as you see, to go on. The nearest breakdown train is at Blayford, and it's not likely that it will be despatched till the morning.   There's not a house anywhere near here, and the best thing we can do is to walk back along the line to Heston Junction.   There's a very fair inn there where you gentlemen can get beds for the night."

Then the Bishop of Frattenbury—dirty, grimy, blood-bespattered—stood forth in his torn, fluttering garments, and spoke.

"I *won't* go back to Heston," he exclaimed.   "I am due to speak at an important meeting at Redminster to-night, and I insist upon your making some arrangements for getting me there.   I *must* be there!"

Hazell looked at him with admiration.   The true British spirit had come out in his lordship—the spirit of pig-headedness that refuses to be daunted by obstacles because it has a grievance against someone.

"I'm very sorry," said the guard, "but I don't see how you're to get to Redminster to-night."

"I tell you I *must* be there," said the Bishop, the marks of episcopacy manifesting themselves despite the mud. "You ought to have guarded against this breakdown, but, since it has occurred, it is your plain duty to devise some plan by which passengers shall reach their destination. I am the principal speaker at this meeting to-night, and in my whole career I have never failed to keep an engagement. I intended catching the 7.30 from Cathfield to Redminster, arriving at the latter place at 7.50, in time for me to reach the hall at 8. It is your duty to assist me to do this."

It was splendid to hear him speak. Even the driver, who was standing by, felt that somehow he had committed a perfectly heinous offence, and, although he was a Baptist by choice, it began to dawn upon him that a Bishop's anathemas might perchance affect Nonconformists in certain cases.

"If it weren't for the broken axle," he said apologetically, "we might get her on the rails with the screw-jack and try running her on."

"Do so," commanded the Bishop, "and, if necessary, proceed without the axle."

"It is absolutely impossible to go on," broke in Thorpe Hazell, "but, if you are determined to speak at this meeting, I might perhaps make a suggestion."

"The officials ought to get me out of the difficulty," replied the Bishop loftily, "but what do you propose?"

"It is now close on seven," said Hazell, "and the distance to Cathfield is nearly four miles along the line. It is out of the question trying to catch the 7.30, but there is a later train which would get you into Redminster by 8.45, and if we started walking at once we might catch it. Perhaps you would allow me to accompany you, as I wish to go on to Redminster myself."

The Bishop thought for a moment.

"Ahem! I suppose it is the only course to take, and I am much obliged to you. But I shall write to the general manager," he went on, turning to the guard.

"Yes, my lord," said that individual meekly.

"We ought to lose no time," said Hazell, "but— er—if we catch that train—your lordship—well, is hardly in a suitable costume to speak at a meeting."

"Dear me!" exclaimed the Bishop, "I never thought of that. How exceedingly unfortunate. I have no change in my bag, either—only my—er— night—attire. But I could possibly borrow a coat from one of the clergy."

"Meanwhile," said Hazell, "if you will allow me, I have a spare jacket I could lend you—just for the walk—that is, if you can get into it."

"You're welcome to my coat," broke in the guard, with the idea of a peace-offering in his mind. "I've another in my van—and I'm about your size."

Finally, the Bishop of Frattenbury took off his coat and tattered apron, and accepted the guard's offer. But he stuck to his own hat, which he had left in the carriage. Then Thorpe Hazell borrowed a lantern from the guard and set off along the track with the Bishop, whilst the others prepared to walk back to Heston.

"I'm afraid you will find it rather a stiff walk," said Hazell. "Might I offer you some refreshments? I seldom travel without them."

"Thank you," replied the Bishop, "but I am a teetotaler."

"The refreshments to which I allude are chocolate and milk," rejoined Hazell.

The Bishop accepted a bit of chocolate, and they stumbled along the centre of the single track in silence for a while. It was rough work, but the Bishop well understood that the catching of the later train at Cathfield meant a quick progress, and that even then it was a mere chance. Yet the prelate was a man of grit, despite his pompous demeanour, and he was determined that the Redminster meeting should not lose his speech on the Education Question if he could help it.

They had gone about a quarter of a mile along the track, Hazell leading the way, and considerately directing the light of the lantern on to the ground so that his companion might best see where to tread, when the former suddenly uttered an exclamation of joy.

The flash of his lantern had fallen upon an object lying beside the line. He stopped short.

"What is it?" asked the Bishop.

"If you're agreeable, I think we might make our progress a bit easier," said Hazell.

"How?"

"Here's a trolley. If we can get it on the line, we could ride on it."

"But how about the motive power? I hardly see——"

"*We* shall have to be the power," broke in Hazell; "and we've not only a stiff wind behind us, but, if I am not very much mistaken, most of the line from here to Cathfield is on a down gradient. Kindly give me a hand!" The Bishop, in some surprise, did as he was asked.

Under Hazell's directions his lordship assisted

him to put the two pairs of wheels on the rails and the heavy frame on to them.   There was a shunter's "coupling staff" among the tackle, and Hazell placed this, together with the lamp, on the trolley.

" Evidently the platelayers have bagged it to push with," he said. " Well, we may find it handy ? Now, then, can you kneel on one knee on that side ? That's right.   I'll take this.   Press your other foot on the ground and give a shove—·so !   Off we go. Can you manage it ? "

" It's work to which I'm scarcely accustomed," said the panting prelate grimly, "but I'll do my best."

" Good ! " replied Hazell, in admiration. " We're picking up speed fast now.   Steady—long strokes, please ! "

The trolley began to run along rapidly. Presently the light of the lamp fell with a passing flash on a short post beside the line, with two arms, one level, and the other at a downward angle.

" A falling gradient ! " cried Hazell. " Climb right on.   That's it ! "

He gave the Bishop a hand while the latter struggled on to the trolley, falling flat as he did so. He clutched his hat with one hand and the edge of the trolley with the other. Hazell knelt, holding the Bishop's coat just at the small of the back to steady him.   The trolley felt the momentum every instant, and was soon running on the down grade quite furiously.

" I—hope—there's—no — danger ! " jerked the Bishop as he bumped.   " If—we—met a—train— I——"

" All right ! " broke in Hazell cheerfully.   " It's a

single line, and our driver had the staff. No other train can run."

The exact meaning was dim to his companion, who gathered, nevertheless, that his fears in this direction were groundless.

"But—suppose the—line's—not—clear—or the—things they—call—points—are not—set—right!"

Hazell laughed.

"Don't worry. There are no points between Heston Junction and Cathfield—not even a station. It's quite safe."

"But—how — can we — stop?" went on the Bishop, as the trolley bounded forward.

"This gradient won't last long, and we can always stop by putting our feet on the rails and pressing—a human brake!"

"I—hope it—won't—end in—a—human breakage!" exclaimed the Bishop, with a grim and noble attempt at humour which went straight to Hazell's heart.

"Good old chap!" he muttered. Presently the speed began to slacken, and the Bishop slowly rose to his knees from his recumbent position. Simultaneously both men broke out into a hearty laugh.

"Enjoying the ride?" asked Hazell.

"I was thinking that some of the younger clergy might enjoy seeing me taking it," remarked the Bishop.

"A coincidence—so was I!"

"Shall we catch that other train?"

Hazell managed to look at his watch.

"Easily! We must push again a bit. I'll use the staff."

He stood upright to do so. The Bishop kicked out manfully once more. As Hazell had said, the wind was behind them, helping them tremendously. They struck another gradient—a long one this time. Hazell looked again at his watch.

"It's rather different from walking," he said. "We shall be in loads of time for the 8.45. That will get us to Redminster a little after nine."

"No chance of catching the 7.30, I suppose?" asked the Bishop.

"No. It's not very far off that time now—and we've the best part of two miles to go. Besides which, the last half mile or more is a steep up gradient, and we shall have to walk it."

They set to pushing again. The line was almost level now. Presently the Bishop exclaimed:

"What's that light?"

Far away, on their right, a sudden flash of radiance had sprung up in the darkness of the black wintry night.

"Opening the coal-box to fire a locomotive," replied Hazell. "And what's more, I'm pretty sure it's the train you wanted to catch running along towards Cathfield. Hullo!" as he caught sight of another gradient post, "there's a steep drop here—one in fifty, if I recollect rightly. Jump on and hold tight! There'll be a curve presently."

The trolly had already begun to gather speed. Even Hazell, who was on the right of the Bishop, had to hold on. Once more the light of the main line train flashed upwards, like a searchlight, and this time Hazell gave vent to an excited "Hullo!"

In order to explain the thought that had suddenly struck him, it will be necessary to give a brief description of the railway at this particular spot. As has been said, the little single line from Heston Junction to Cathfield was about seven miles in length.   From about two miles beyond the scene of the breakdown it bore round gradually to the left, until at length it met the main line at a point a little over a mile from Cathfield.

But this point was not a junction.   That is to say, the single line, instead of crossing on to the main by facing points controlled by a signal-box in the angle, ran parallel on the left of the main track all the way to Cathfield, where it had its own little "bay" terminus.

This arrangement, involving a little more capital expenditure at first, had its advantages in that the necessity for a "junction-box" and the maintenance of its signalman was obviated, thus making it cheaper in the long run.   Similar instances may occur to the reader, as, for example, the running of the Midhurst single line from Fishbourne to Chichester alongside the up main South Coast track; or the bit of the Abingdon branch that runs parallel with the main down Great Western for some little distance into Radley.   The arrangement, also, has another advantage in leaving both main and branch lines absolutely clear at all times.

Now the trolley, rushing downwards at fairly high speed, was just approaching the point from which it would continue running close along the main up track.   And on this main up track, further away from the point, the express, that would ultimately stop at Cathfield, came thundering along. They were, naturally, in front of her, and Hazell knew by her head-lights, which just appeared in view—a green light above a white—that she was the train in question.

"Hullo!" he shouted, as a sudden idea took possession of him.

" What's—the—matter ? " cried the Bishop, who was on the jerk again.

Hazell's reply was unintelligible to his lord-ship.

" The tail-lights of the branch train are a red *and* a white, but the main-line trains carry a red light only ! "

" What—on—earth——"

" Hold *on !* "

They came swinging round the curve with a clatter, and then the light of the lamp glanced on the shining up rail parallel with them and some five feet from the right edge of the trolley.

Hazell looked back. The head-lights of the express were out of sight now, there being a bit of a curve on the main line. Kneeling upright, as well as the shaking trolley would let him, Hazell took up the guard's lamp and turned the red shade on. Then he hooked its handle to the hook on the end of the coupling staff.

" Hold on to the edge with your left hand, my lord ! Right ! Now take my left hand with your other. Don't let go, for goodness' sake. Good ! Here she comes. Just in time ! "

Holding the coupling staff with his right hand, he reached it out, till the lantern was just over the middle of the parallel up track, the red light point-ing back towards the approaching train.

" What—are—you—doing ? "

" Trying to get you in time for your meeting ! " replied Hazell. " Hold on. We're nearly on the level now."

As the driver of the express came round the slight curve, he saw the red tail-light, apparently of an up main line train, for it was on his track, moving on in front of him. Instantly he shut off steam and whistled furiously.

And then, as Hazell glanced back, he saw the sparks flying under the train, and he knew that the Westinghouse brake was doing its work.

"I can manage by myself now," he cried, for the trolley was slackening speed. "Stop her, my lord!"

Very gingerly the Bishop applied the brake—to wit, his episcopal boot—and slowly they came to a standstill. So did the train—not fifty yards behind.

The front guard jumped from his van and came running forward, expecting to see a train—or, at least, a detached truck in the way. When he caught sight of the trolley and the two men on the other rail, his indignation expressed itself in pretty strong language as he inquired what they meant by it. Hazell briefly explained the breakdown and how they had journeyed on.

"But, why the —— did you stop my train, even if your story's true?"

"Because," said Hazell imperturbably, "my friend the Bishop here did not wish to lose his connection."

"Bishop be——" began the guard, as he turned his lantern on the prelate.

"Hush!" checked Hazell, "his lordship is un-accustomed to such language."

"A pretty Bishop!" sneered the guard, as he looked at the extraordinary figure. "But you'll have to pay for this!"

"Oh, no," replied Hazell sweetly. "We've both got first-class tickets. But we're wasting precious time. Clear this trolley off—we're coming with you."

"And I will see that you are properly recompensed," said the Bishop loftily, recovering something of his episcopal dignity.

They went on in the guard's van. At Cathfield Hazell explained matters to the stationmaster, who was getting anxious about the non-arrival of the branch train.

"You'll have to settle with the authorities for stopping the train," he said, as Hazell gave him his card.

"Oh, I think that will be easy enough—I've done one or two little amateur jobs for the G.M." replied the railway expert ; " he knows me very well."

The run on to Redminster was in a first-class carriage.

"Let me thank you exceedingly for all your trouble," said the Bishop, who was still attired in the guard's coat. "How can I repay you for it ? "

"Easily," replied Hazell. "May I refer to our former conversation—just after we left Heston ? "

" Certainly."

"You appeared to be sceptical as to the food values of oatmeal, macaroni, Dutch cheese, and lentils. It would be such a pleasure to me, my lord, if you would lose that scepticism, after personal experience."

" I don't quite understand."

" If, in return for any small service I have rendered, you would try these foods exclusively, with the exception of milk as a beverage, for, say a fortnight, I'm sure you would be convinced."

His lordship pressed his lips and frowned, but the frown soon developed into a grim smile.

" Very well," he said, " I *will*."

" And you will let me know ? "

" I will let you know."

5—Stories of the Railway.

"Thank you, my lord. Ah, here we are at Redminster. But you cannot speak in that costume?"

"I shall drive straight to the Deanery first, and borrow some clothes from the Dean. I am staying the night there."

At a quarter past eight the Bishop of Frattenbury, rigidly clad—a little *too* rigidly, perhaps, for the Dean was the sparer man of the two—was addressing a crowded meeting at the Redminster Town Hall as only his lordship, who was famed for platform eloquence, could.

 *   *   *   *   *   *

And here followed the postscript, after the lapse of a couple of weeks.

> The Palace,
> Frattenbury.

My Dear Sir,

I have faithfully kept my promise to you, and strictly adhered to the abominable diet you prescribed for a fortnight—which ends to-night. I am much looking forward to resuming my ham for breakfast to-morrow, and rejoice that Providence provided the necessary animal for its production. I am still more than grateful to you for your kind and shrewd services on the eventful evening when I first made your acquaintance, and should you ever be in Frattenbury, hope that you will remember that the Apostle has enjoined bishops to be "given to hospitality." You shall, on that occasion, have your four abominable (the word suits admirably) foods *ad lib.*, but you will find me carnivorous.

> Believe me,
> Yours very truly,
> G. Frattenbury.

VIII

THE ADVENTURE OF THE PILOT ENGINE

WHEN a special train is to be run on our railways, papers of directions are printed and issued to station-masters and others. These contain minute details concerning the timing of the run, and the keeping of the line clear, how this train is to be shunted into a refuge siding at one station, and that train has to be kept clear at another point.

In the case of any important or Royal personage travelling, these instructions are marked "private," and are jealously guarded.

Some three years ago, at a juncture when European politics were considered by diplomatists to be in a very delicate state, an announcement might have been seen in several Continental papers to this effect: "Count von Neglein, being slightly indisposed owing to his arduous duties, has retired for a few days, under the direction of his physician, to his country house at B——. He hopes to be able to resume work in a week's time."

At the same time, a messenger from Downing Street called upon the general manager of the London and East Midland Railway and gave him an order with strict injunctions that the matter was to be kept private.

A special train was required the following Tuesday to run from London to Singlehurst. Every precaution was to be taken for the safety of this train, as a most important person was going to travel by it. The general manager immediately summoned the superintendent of the line, and before the morning was out a proof of the "special working instructions" had been laid on his desk, damp from the company's printers.

That same morning three men were closeted together in a house in the West End of London. Two of them were of a distinctly foreign appearance, the third might have belonged to any nationality. He was a man of medium height, clean-shaven, with close-cut hair, ordinary features, and mild-looking grey eyes. The only thing of any note about his face was a certain set and resolute compression of his lips.

The language in which the trio were speaking was French, and the subject under discussion was that of Count von Neglein's little indisposition.

"The news is of the gravest character," said the elder of the two foreign-looking men. "There can be no doubt about it that if Count von Neglein has an interview with the English Prime Minister in the presence of the King during the ensuing week our plans will be frustrated completely."

"You are sure that your information is correct?" asked the other man.

"Positively. Besides, Dubourg here can corroborate it," and he turned to the third man.

"Quite correct," said Dubourg. "The Continental journey will be made to Ostend, and thence to London by private boat. These little steam yachts are handy."

" There is no possibility of, er—persuading the Count to relinquish his journey on the Continent or by sea ? " said the first speaker, with a curious interrogatory lift of his eyebrows.

" None," replied Dubourg. " The arrangements are excellent—for them."

" Well, *you* ought to know something about that," said the second man.

Dubourg bowed slightly.

" It is my business," he said.

" The King," went on the first speaker, who was evidently the one in authority—" the King is staying with the Duke of Worcester, and will be there all next week. Singlehurst, I believe, is the nearest station. The Prime Minister and the French Ambassador are invited there to dine on Monday. That means staying the night."

" And that yacht will arrive early on Tuesday morning," put in Dubourg.

" Exactly. Well—er—my instructions are to prevent an interview between von Neglein and the Prime Minister at all costs. Now, Dubourg, what have you to say ? "

Dubourg thought for a minute, his lips tightly compressed.

" We must find out," he said presently, " how he is going to travel from London to Singlehurst. If it is an ordinary train, as you know, I have done something in this line before. But if it is a special —well ! "

" Well ? "

" It may be a question of stopping at nothing."

" Then stop at nothing," said the chief coldly. " If he is removed altogether, so much the better for our interests."

" I will make inquiries and see you this evening,"
said Dubourg rising.

" Do so. Good-morning. A most excellent
person this Dubourg," he went on to his companion, " he has been an engineer and an actor,
and he knows ten European languages fluently. If
the thing's to be done at all, he's the man to do it
—especially if it is a question of railways. That's
his chief line."

The same evening Dubourg called again at the
West End house. A dinner party was in progress,
and the elder of the two foreigners sat at the head
of the table, an order across his breast, and was
addressed with much deference by his guests. As
soon as the servant handed him Dubourg's card, he
begged to be excused for a few moments, and left
the table.

" Well ? " he said to Dubourg, when they were
seated in his private room.

Dubourg laid a printed paper on the table.

" It was difficult to get," he said, " but fortunately the printers were open to a fee."

The paper, which was marked " Strictly Private,"
was headed :

" Instructions for working special train from
London to Singlehurst."

Then followed a long list of details. The train
itself was to leave the London terminus at 8.30 a.m.,
preceded by a pilot engine at 8.20.

" They are taking extra precautions with that
pilot engine," remarked Dubourg, with a light
laugh.

The other looked at him narrowly.

" Why do you smile ? "

" Because I think it would have been as well for

Count von Neglein's restoration to health if they had not determined to run a pilot."

" It is going to be a serious affair ? "

" Very serious. And dangerous—that is, if my plan is successful."

" And your plan ? "

" No," replied Dubourg, " I won't give you the details, lest I should fail. But the key to it lies here."

And he put his finger on a paragraph of the " Instructions."

The other read :

" Inspector Inglis will travel on the engine of the express, which will be worked by Driver Forbes and Fireman Scott. The pilot engine will be worked by Driver Fraser and Fireman Norris."

" Four of the best enginemen on the line," remarked Dubourg. " I happened to see Driver Fraser and Fireman Norris bring a train in to-day— excellent men ! "

" I don't see your point, but I know I can trust you. Koravitch, who was with us this morning, will give you any funds or assistance."

" I shall want the latter. To-morrow I am going to make certain inquiries about Fireman Norris. I've taken quite a fancy to the look of him. On Monday I shall take a journey down the line, merely to refresh my memory of a few details. I shall be back that evening. If my little plan succeeds, I don't think there will be any interview. Good-night ! "

*   *   *   *   *   *

Late on Monday evening, Dubourg sat in his lodgings poring over a rough map of a section of the London and East Midland line that he had made as the result of his trip that day, and referring closely to the "Special Working Instructions" that lay beside it on the table.

The first fifty miles of the London and East Midland consist of a quadruple track, the two main lines on the left for up and down fast trains, and the others "relief lines" for slow trains. There are places where a train can cross from the main line to the relief, or *vice versa*, the points being, of course, controlled by signal-boxes; and there are also places where, for shunting purposes, trains can cross from the down line to the up, or *vice versa*, but in this case they must first stop and then reverse.

Thirty-five miles down the line is Rushwood Station. Two and a-half miles further is Alton Siding Box, which commands crossing points on the relief line only, the main line metals being clear. Five miles on is Holt Box, where points are so arranged that trains may cross in all the ways I have mentioned. Half-a-mile further is the long Roxton Tunnel, with a signal-box at the entrance.

When a train has passed the Roxton Box the

Map showing the scene of Dubourg's plot.

man on duty signals " line clear " to Holt, and the
signalman at Holt is free to admit a train on his
section from Alton Siding Box.

In the case of very special trains, such as those
carrying Royalty, and when a pilot engine is used,
all traffic on the adjacent line must come to a
standstill between the passage of the " pilot " and
the " special " following it; while, with regard to
trains running in the same direction on relief lines,
a stop must be made for extra precaution wherever
there is a crossing-over place, when the " special "
is timed to run by on the main line just at that
moment.

The two special notices which Dubourg was
studying so intensely were these :

" Directions to the signalman on duty at Holt
Box. Light engine No. 321, running on the up
line to Rushwood, must stop opposite box, and the
9.5 local down passenger train from Rushwood
must be stopped outside facing points on relief line
during passing of pilot and special." A " light
engine," by the way, is an engine running by itself.

The man called Koravitch came in presently and
glanced at the map.

" Well, Dubourg," he said, " is everything·
ready ? "

" So far as it can be," replied the other. " There
are several weak spots in the plan, but I must trust
to luck. And here is the weakest, I think."

He laid his finger on the rough map at the point
marking the Roxton Tunnel Box.

" As for myself," he went on, " it is a risky thing.
After our little business of to-morrow morning you
must start off with the motor. I want you to be
waiting a little after nine on the main road just

outside the village of Roxton, on the London side.
Are all the other things ready?"

"Yes."

"The carriage?"

"Yes. Our men are warned."

"Good! Then we'll have some rest. Six
o'clock to-morrow, mind. It'll be quite dark then."

*   *   *   *   *   *

About half-a-mile from the terminus of the
London and East Midland Railway are a couple of
streets of small houses belonging to the company,
and entirely occupied by railwaymen. You may
see them going in and out of their houses at all
hours of the day or night. Drivers and firemen
starting to "work" trains to the Midlands, goods
brakesmen returning after a weary run up, smart
guards, dingy engine-cleaners, the rank and file of
the great railway army.

It was pitch dark on the morning of the eventful
Tuesday, when a closed carriage drove up to one of
these little houses, and a man, with his cap drawn
down over his face, sprang out and rapped violently
at the door. The people were well accustomed to
these sudden calls, especially in foggy weather. A
minute later and a window opened, and a head
appeared at it.

"Who's there?"

"Mr. Walters," growled the man below. "I
want Norris at once."

"I'm Norris, sir."

"Sharp, then. You're firing the pilot for the
special?"

"Yes, sir; but she don't start till 8.20."

"There's an alteration. Quick! Put on your
clothes and hurry up!"

The window was shut down, and in a very few minutes Norris came out of the house, clad in his working clothes and ready for the "run," his little bag with provisions and the familiar blue tea-can in his hand.

"There's not a moment to lose," said the supposed Mr. "Walters," holding the door of the cab open. "Jump in—Fraser has gone on."

Norris got into the cab, and Dubourg, for it was he, followed. The driver whipped up his horse, and before the unfortunate fireman had realised what was happening, he found himself in the grasp of two powerful men, who snicked a pair of hand-cuffs on his wrists, and then proceeded to gag him.

"Now, if you keep still," said Dubourg, "we won't hurt you; but, if you make any resistance or refuse to do what we tell you, I can't answer for the consequences."

They drove along at a furious pace, and presently drew up at a house in Camden Town, the door of which opened immediately. Dubourg and Koravitch took the fireman by the arms and hurried him into the house, the door was closed by a third man, and the cab drove off.

The room into which they carried Norris was brilliantly lighted, and a looking-glass stood on the table. Dubourg lost no time.

"We're going to trouble you for your clothes, my friend," he said quietly, "and then you shall enjoy a rest."

In ten minutes the fireman had his outer clothes stripped from him and Dubourg had put them on. Then he opened a small tin case, took out a wig, some false hair, spirit gum, and other make-up materials, and set to work on his own face, carefully studying first Norris and then the reflection in the looking-glass. In a very short time he was transformed into the exact likeness of the fireman. By this time Koravitch had gone, but not before he had assisted the other man in binding Norris securely.

" Now," said Dubourg to Norris, as he put a small life-preserver in his own pocket and carefully examined a revolver, " you'll suffer no inconvenience beyond remaining here for a few hours. A letter will be posted to your wife stating where you are, and she'll receive it this afternoon. I'm sorry to leave you gagged, but there are neighbours who might hear you."

With that he walked out of the house with his fellow-conspirators.

  *   *   *   *   *   *

Dubourg went his way to the engine-sheds of the London and East Midland Railway to all appearances an ordinary fireman, returning nods of greeting which were given him by men he met.

He had served in the secret service of a powerful European nation for ten years now, and his chief work had been in connection with railways, steamers, and other methods of travelling. Railways and their working were his speciality, and to a man who had driven locomotives scores of times, the details of a fireman's work were nothing. He knew exactly what was required, and gave in his name at the check office with as much unconcern as if he had been Norris himself, glancing at the notice board with quite a practised eye.

Fraser had arrived before him, and, lamp and oil-can in hand, was in the pit beneath the great engine, carefully inspecting every portion of the works. He gave a nod to his mate presently, as he joined him on the foot-plate ; it was dark inside the engine-shed, and he did not notice anything strange.

Afterwards Dubourg took care to keep his face turned away from him as far as possible, besides which, it was a gloomy winter's morning, and men on the footplate have too much to do to look narrowly into each other's faces. Their eyes are fixed on other things, and driver and firemen on duty are not talkers. A dozen words in a hundred miles' run is often as much as they exchange.

Presently they "whistled up" to be run off the shed road, backed down to the "special," and stood at the end of the platform ready to start. Dubourg forgot nothing. He saw that the tail-light was properly fixed on the back of the tender—there were tunnels on the route—he placed the special head discs, denoting the character of the engine, in front of the smoke-box, and when a loco. inspector strolled up to the engine, he gave a twist to the hand-brake in the most approved manner.

Punctually to the minute they moved out. Dubourg stood slightly behind the driver, carefully noting the pressure-gauge, the needle of which soon began to move up as the blast operated. Directly the steam began to "blow off" at the valve he was ready for coaling. In a few seconds, as the needle began to go up once more, he commenced to put the feed on by setting the injector to work, screwing down the water-regulating wheel with such easy method and adjustment, that the driver's suspicions were never once aroused.

So the "pilot" ran on.

A dozen words had not been exchanged between the two men, so perfect was the working of both. Exactly at scheduled time they passed Rushwood, and the pseudo-fireman began to keep a sharp look out on his own account. At Holt Box he noted, with much satisfaction, that the local train stood on the " down relief," and the light engine on the " up main," according to instructions.

The half mile on to Roxton commenced with a sharp curve after leaving Holt, and through a deep cutting. One more coaling operation, and Dubourg had his hand in his pocket, grasping the life-preserver.

The instant the train had entered the tunnel he acted. With his left hand he dashed off Fraser's cap, standing behind him, and at the same moment, struck him on the top of the head with his weapon. The driver, stunned with the blow, fell on the foot-plate like a log. Dubourg sprang to the regulator, shut off steam, and then put on the brake, the engine coming to a standstill in the tunnel.

Now came the ticklish part of his dastardly plan, and well he knew it. The signalman he had just passed at the mouth of the tunnel was like a sentry, to be overcome by foul means, before he could attain his object. But Doubourg was a man absolutely devoid of either fear or feeling.

Reversing his engine, he slowly backed out of the tunnel, stopping before the box, to the intense surprise of its occupant. The latter came rushing out on to the platform outside his door, first glancing to see that his signals were set against the " special."

" What's up ? " he cried.

" This ! " shouted Dubourg.

There was a sharp crack as his hand flew up with something glittering in it. The signalman staggered to his door, but fell on the threshold. Dubourg, calm as ever, lifted the insensible form of the driver and dropped him beside the track. Then he threw open the regulator and jumped off himself.

The engine began to move backwards.

Very coolly Dubourg mounted the steps of the signal box. He stooped to look at the man.

"H'm! Don't think I've killed him," he muttered.

Then he went into the box, deliberately selected an instrument, and gave the signal "Line clear" back to Holt Box.

And all the time that pilot engine was running back on the very metals over which the special was approaching. The signal that would have been given by the man on duty would have warned his colleague at Holt in time for him to clear off the light engine which stood there to the "up relief," and cross the runaway engine over to the "up main." The next moment Dubourg was running across country to catch his motor and escape.

*   *   *   *   *   *

The signalman at Holt Box stood in front of his instruments, expecting every moment the sharp ring on his bell warning him from Alton Siding that the special was passing that point and entering upon the section between them. He never dreamt of any danger, having received the signal from Roxton Box that the line ahead was perfectly clear beyond that point.

Suddenly he heard a roar and a rattle round the curve and, as he glanced in that direction, his horrified gaze met the runaway pilot engine. Never was signalman placed in such an awful dilemma. The immediate danger crowded all else from his mind as he grasped a lever.

There flashed before him this :

If he set the crossing-points the pilot would crash into the light engine on the "up main." If he set the other points it would come into collision with the passenger train standing on the "down relief." There were but a few seconds in which to choose either course, and in his hesitation he lost them. The engine ran by both sets of points. At that moment there came the signal from Alton Siding Box :

"Train entering section."

Dubourg had made his calculations with diabolical cunning. For even if the special had not passed Alton Box, and it had been possible to stop her there, unless she could have pulled up and backed into Rushwood in time, which was hardly likely, the smash would still have taken place, there being no crossing points at Alton over which the runaway engine could be switched.

The case stood thus : The special, with Count von Neglein aboard her, and the pilot engine were rushing towards each other on a five-mile stretch of line with absolutely no possibility of changing metals, the former travelling at fifty and the latter at forty miles an hour. Surely it seemed that Dubourg's diabolical plot could never be frustrated by human means.

But it was, through a page-boy in the first instance, and through Thorpe Hazell in the actual working.

It came about in this way. Hazell had had in his employment a sharp boy named Sam Thorne. Making a change, however, in his domestic establishment which led to the employment of an older servant instead, this page-boy had left him and had taken a situation in a large boarding-house in Bloomsbury, the very house, as it happened, where Dubourg had his apartments.

On the Monday night when Dubourg was discussing affairs with Koravitch, Sam Thorne came into the room with some hot water and glasses. He overheard Dubourg make a remark in which he caught the words " Holt Signal Box," and his quick eye caught sight of the map of the railway which was lying on the table and the words "Special Working Instructions" on the paper beside it. Neither of the men dreamt that the boy had noticed anything.

Now, while he had been in service with Hazell, Sam Thorne had gained a great admiration for his master as a railway expert, especially as, on one occasion, he had been made use of in finding out some little detail. He knew well how much Hazell loved getting hold of any mystery of the line.

The idea that something was up struck him forcibly, the fact that Dubourg had asked to be called at five o'clock exciting his suspicions. He was a boy of strong imagination and of action, so he determined to put Hazell on the track. For this purpose he begged paper and envelope of the cook, and scrawled the following effusion :

DEAR SIR,

Two furrin men staying here are up to something to-morrow—I think about railways. Is there a place called Holt Signal Box on the London and East Midland ? And they were looking at speshul working instruckshuns. I saw them, and I thought Ide let you no. Yours truely,

SAM THORNE.

It was nearly ten o'clock. Sam asked leave to

post his letter, and as soon as he was outside the house he started off for Hazell's flat, taking a 'bus on the way. Here he found that Hazell was out of town, but had left his address with the porter. He was staying in the country at Holmfield.

"Better post it if it's particular. He'll get it to-morrow morning," said the man.

"It's very particular," replied the boy. "Give us a stamp, gov'nor."

He posted the letter, and received an awful wigging when he got back at half-past eleven. But he felt, somehow, that he had done his duty—even if the letter arrived too late.

As a matter of fact, Hazell got it at breakfast the next morning. He read it with a smile at first. Then he suddenly remembered that an official had told him the previous Saturday that a very important special was to be run that morning on the L. and E.M. He did not know, of course, who was to travel in it, but the mention of "two furrin men" aroused his suspicions.

Holmfield was a village in the heart of the country, devoid of railway or telegraph. But there was one point about the place—it was within fifteen miles of Roxton, and not much further, therefore, from Holt Box.

"Weston," exclaimed Hazell to his host, pulling out his watch at the same time, "you will have to excuse me, but this letter has disturbed me greatly. Will you lend me your bicycle and a local map? I want to be off in ten minutes."

The other, rather surprised, acquiesced, and in ten minutes Hazell was pedalling for all he was worth on the Roxton Road, keen on discovery, but little dreaming what was before him.

After riding some fifteen miles he deviated from the main road by a turning that his map showed him would lead him along the line close by Holt Box. He reached the top of a little hill commanding a view of the railway, and as he did so he saw the pilot engine run through. He could also discern the stationary train and light engine, and these facts told him at once that the engine running through must be the pilot of a special. He wondered, as he rode on, whether anything really was likely to happen, or whether he had only had a false alarm. Presently he arrived opposite Holt Box—which was on the further side of the line— got off his bicycle, and climbed the railing. He was now exactly opposite the light engine.

At that moment he saw what the terrified signal-man had grasped—the reversed pilot engine running back. He even heard the two strokes of the bell that announced to his practised ear the entering of the special on the same section, and he knew in an instant the awful danger. An idea swept upon him like an inspiration. Dashing over the metals he made for the light engine, climbed the foot-plate, and cried to the astonished driver :

" Open the regulator—quick—brakes off, fireman. We can save her ! "

He had seized the regulator himself as he spoke, and the engine had already begun to move, the fireman mechanically taking off the brake, the driver standing dumb-stricken.

"*Overtake her !*" yelled Hazell, pointing towards the retreating pilot.

Then the driver grasped his meaning.

" It's an awful risk," he cried, as he took the regulator, " steady, mate "—to the fireman—" don't coal her, man, yet—for Heaven's sake. We shall want all our steam."

"How long have we got?" asked Hazell.

"Two minutes at the outside," replied the man; "will you do it, sir—or shall I?"

"I will."

"It's dangerous—fearful."

"I know. Go on!"

The driver carefully "notched up" with his reversing wheel, and got her out of "full throw" as the speed increased. The pilot had a fair start, and nearly six hundred yards separated them now. He and Hazell looked grimly ahead. The distance between the engines gradually grew less. The driver glanced at his watch.

"Half a minute gone!"

Then he muttered:

"She's not running more than forty; she's in full gear, thank God!"

Which means that the pilot's cylinders were fully open to steam, and that, at the speed at which she was running, the strokes of the piston were somewhat retarded.

Another thirty seconds passed in anxious silence. At length there were only fifty yards between the engines.

"Look out, sir!" cried the driver.

"What are you going to do, sir?" asked the fireman, speaking for the first time.

"Jump!" said Hazell.

"You *can't*, sir!"

"I'll try, anyway," replied Hazell, going to the side. Twenty seconds more and the two engines were running side by side.

"Keep her so, driver! Steady!"

At length the footplates were opposite, some three feet of space separating them. Hazell grasped the handrails and calculated the distance. Then he gave a forward spring, and landed fair on the pilot's step, clutching at her handrail.

"Thank God!" he cried as he flew at the regulator, closed it, and turned on the brake.

Then he glanced over his shoulder.

Not a quarter of a mile behind the special suddenly came round a slight curve. There was a furious whistling, then the white steam was shut off, and a minute later the train had stopped, barely a hundred yards from the engine that had so nearly destroyed her.

*   *   *   *   *   *

The affair was hushed up. The loco. inspector and Driver Hicks, of the light engine, went forward with the pilot, while the light engine was run on to Rushwood by her fireman. Hazell accompanied him, and took train to Roxton to recover his bicycle —walking out to Holt Box afterwards.

Von Neglein only knew that "a block had occurred on the line," and his views of English railways were rather lowered in consequence.

The signalman at Roxton and the driver of the pilot both recovered, an important treaty was duly signed, and a "diplomatic triumph" ensued.

Dubourg was never discovered, in fact, the police received an intimation that it was useless to pursue their "clues," and the railway officials in high places were also advised to hold their tongues. So they did. As to Hazell, he was warmly thanked by the superintendent of the line, and Driver Hicks was substantially rewarded for the part he had played in what might have been an awful tragedy.

IX

THE STOLEN NECKLACE

THORPE HAZELL was dining at his club. They were accustomed to his eccentricities there, and hardly a member had looked up from his newspaper when he had divested himself of his coat, and gravely gone through his "digestive exercises" in a convenient corner before proceeding to the dining-room. Here preparation had been made, for he had told the head-waiter he was coming. A table was reserved, and on it stood a carafe of milk, a little loaf of brown bread, and a dish of his favourite biscuits. A bowl—he never would use a soup-plate—of lentil soup was soon put before him, and he commenced his meal.

"Hullo, Hazell," said a voice presently, as the speaker clapped him on the shoulders, "don't you overfeed yourself, old chap!"

"Oh, it's you, is it, Masters?" exclaimed Hazell, as he looked up. "I thought you were out of town."

"So I was till half-an-hour ago. I've just come up by the West-Northern, and I'm frantically hungry. Thought I'd come round for a meal at once before going to my chambers."

Hazell motioned him to take a seat at his table. The waiter came up and presented the menu. Hazell listened while his friend ordered dinner. Then he said:

"Oxtail soup is very heating. Whiting is a fish

that ought to be cooked within two hours of catching. Curry is deadly for the liver. How you can digest Welsh rarebit is more than I can imagine, and alcohol in any form has been proved by the leading doctors to be a poison."

Frank Masters laughed heartily.

" Your life must be a misery to you, Hazell ! "

" Not at all. I never suffer from indigestion."

" Neither do I."

" Not now, perhaps, but your old age will be a misery to you."

" How do you know yours won't, too ? You haven't put *that* to the test with your system yet ! "

Hazell shook his head sadly as the other fell to on his soup. There were few converts to be made at the club.

" Did you have a good run up to town ? " asked Hazell presently.

" Capital."

" Where did you come from ? "

" Redminster."

" Ah, you took the express arriving in town at 7.28 ? "

" Yes, Mr. Bradshaw ! "

" Mr. Bradshaw " was Thorpe Hazell's nickname at the club, and he rather rejoiced in it than otherwise. No man ever attempted the fag of looking at a railway guide when Hazell was near at hand.

" Was it in to time ? "

" To the minute."

" Generally is. Did you notice whether a compound drew it ? "

" What ? "

" A compound locomotive."

" My dear fellow, I haven't the slightest idea what

you mean. As long as I get to my journey's end I don't worry about the engine. Jolly good train, that express. No stop at all except at Wisden Junction, and I can't see the necessity for that."

" They take tickets there," replied Hazell.

" I know. But why the johnny can't collect 'em on the train instead of only just looking at 'em is one of those railway mysteries that you know more about than I do."

" They could collect them on the train, of course," replied Hazell, " or even at Redminster. But there's another reason why the train stops at Wisden—in case there are any passengers for South London."

" Then why do they disturb you on the train, and make you hunt in all your pockets just to see your ticket ? "

" They don't," said Hazell, in blunt contradiction, as he helped himself liberally to boiled rice—for his second course had just arrived.

" But I tell you they do," replied his friend.

" Oh, well," said Hazell, " it must be something new. I travelled by that train a fortnight ago, and they didn't do it then. Oh—what an ass I am! Of course, I know what it was. A ticket inspector must have been on the train. The railway companies are not so foolish as you think, Masters, and they often catch fellows in that way."

The conversation took a general turn, and, after a bit, Hazell finished his meal and said good-night to his friend, with another gentle remonstrance against the savoury he was enjoying.

The next morning he had scarcely finished breakfast at his flat when there came a ring, and he heard his servant show someone into his study. The next moment he was looking at a visiting card.

" Miss St. John Mallaby."

When he went into the study he found himself confronted by a remarkably pretty young lady, whose face, however, was wearing a very anxious expression.

"I hope you don't mind my coming here, Mr. Hazell," she began, "but I think you've met my brother."

"Do sit down," he answered, "yes, of course I have."

" He told me about you, and what a clever railway detective you are, and I've come to you. I thought you might advise me."

Hazell smiled.

"I'm afraid I have a reputation that I don't deserve," he said. " I'm scarcely a railway detective, as you put it."

"Oh, but you *will* help me—please!" said the girl earnestly.

" Of course, I'll do anything I can for you, Miss Mallaby. But tell me what it's about?"

"I don't want anyone to know—I mean I want you to promise you won't tell anyone. I'm in great trouble. I've done something awfully wrong, and it's like a judgment on me."

" My dear young lady," replied Hazell gravely, "before you make a confidant of me are you sure that it is wise to do so?"

"Oh, yes—yes—yes. Because you may be able to help me. Please let me tell you."

" Very well, then," said Hazell encouragingly.

" Well, I've lost a diamond necklace!" she blurted out.

Hazell nodded and waited.

" I ought not to have worn it all," she went on, "and that's the terrible part of it. It belongs to my aunt. I'm staying at her house in town. You see it's going to be mine one day—she has promised to give it to me when I come of age, and that's why I borrowed it."

"Suppose," said Hazell kindly, "you begin at the beginning and try to tell me exactly what has happened?"

"Yes, I will, as well as I can. My mother and I came up last week to stay with aunt for the season. It was then that she showed me the necklace. I'd often heard about it, for it's been in the family a long time. Well, last Monday aunt had to go away unexpectedly, owing to her brother being taken ill. She left her keys in charge of mother. On Tuesday I was to go down to Appledon to Sir Roland Hartingford's. His daughter, who is a great friend of mine, came of age that day, and there was a ball at the house. Just before I started, the idea suddenly struck me that I would dearly love to wear the necklace at the dance. I know it was awfully wrong of me, but the temptation was a strong one, and I found myself saying that if aunt had been at home she would have lent me the diamonds. And then I yielded and took them."

"How did you get them?"

"It was very simple. I had to borrow my mother's keys for something, and she gave me her chatelaine. In it were the other keys. Almost before I realised what I had done, I had gone into my aunt's room and unlocked the safe which is fixed there. The necklace was in a small leather case. I took it out, locked up the safe again, and gave my mother back the keys."

"Did you tell her what you had done?"

"No. She does not know even yet."

" Where did you put the necklace ? "

" In my dressing-case, which contains my own jewellery and which never leaves me when I travel. Well, I went down to Appledon with my maid and wore the diamonds at the ball. It was on the return journey—yesterday—that I lost them."

" In the train ? "

" Yes. That's why I came to you, Mr. Hazell. At least, I think it *must* have been in the train—and yet—I hardly know what to say. It is all so terrible."

" Well, you must try to tell me."

The girl thought for a moment.

" Appledon is on a branch line," she said, " and you join the main line at Redminster."

" Quite so," said Hazell indulgently.

" It must have happened in the main line train, because after we had got in I wanted something from my case and unlocked it. The necklace was there then ; I'm positive of that."

" What train was it ? "

" The 5.40 express from Redminster. I was travelling with my maid in a first-class compartment. It was a corridor train."

" Was anyone else in the carriage with you ? "

The girl hesitated and blushed slightly. Then she said :

" One of the guests at Appledon—Mr. Kestron—was coming up to town by the same train, and he travelled with me."

" The Honourable George Kestron ? "

" Yes."

" I know him slightly," replied Hazell, remembering that a rumour was abroad to the effect that this same Kestron was rather hard up—had borrowed money, so it was said.

Miss Mallaby noticed a certain tone in Hazell's voice as he replied.

"No—*no!*" she exclaimed, "I *can't* suspect him.'

"Had you, then?" asked Hazell.

"The thought *would* come into my head. It was partly for that reason that I did not go to the police. Oh, Mr. Hazell, I don't know *what* to think."

"Well, go on with your story, please. Perhaps you will tell me how you were seated in the carriage?"

She explained that she was at first seated in the corner next to the corridor with her back to the engine, and Kestron was opposite. Her maid was on her left by the window, with the dressing-case, covered over by a rug, between them. After a while, Kestron had suggested changing places, as she had said something about travelling with her back to the engine. She was careful to move the dressing-case over to her side. Afterwards Kestron had changed his place again and had sat next to her until Wisden Junction was reached—the dressing-case being between them.

"Have you known Mr. Kestron long?" asked Hazell.

"I had only met him a few times before the ball. We danced a good deal together that night, but I had not known him very long—that was why I asked my maid to stay in the compartment."

"How came he to travel with you?"

"He had asked me the night before what train I was going by."

"I see. Well, when did you miss the necklace?"

She told him it was after the train had left Wisden Junction. She put her hand into the outside pocket of the case, where she kept her purse, and discovered, to her horror, that a long slit had been cut through the inner side. She unlocked the case, and the necklace was missing. Kestron had got out at Wisden, having to take a train from there on business before he went home that night.

" Do you know his address ? " asked Hazell.

" Lancaster Crescent—number eight, I think."

Having discovered the loss of the jewels, she was terribly upset, and even asked her maid if she had taken them. The latter was indignant, and wanted to be searched on the spot. They looked everywhere in the compartment. It was still broad daylight, and she was certain that neither of them had left the compartment between Redminster and Wisden.

" Did anyone else come in ? "

" No—even the ticket-collector only opened the door, and stood half outside when he asked to see our tickets."

Hazell suddenly remembered that the friend with whom he had been dining on the previous evening had travelled by the same train. He thought for a minute, and then asked her to tell him how the three were seated when the ticket-collector came, and who gave him the tickets.

" Mr. Kestron was next to me—it was after he had changed places the second time. I handed his ticket to the man, who glanced at it and returned it. My maid had both our tickets—she always sees to that—and she showed them to him."

" But as she was near the window, how did she do it ? "

" Why," exclaimed the girl rather petulantly, " she naturally moved across to him."

"I see," said Hazell thoughtfully. "The corridor, of course, was on the *left* as you faced the engine. Can you remember whether the ticket-collector came from the front or back of the train, and whereabouts your carriage was in the train?"

"About the middle. The collector came from the front, but he had passed along the corridor just before."

"Only *just* before?"

"Yes."

"Ah! Well, I think you've told me all I want to know. It's a troublesome case. By the way, what happened when you arrived at the terminus?"

"My aunt's brougham was there to meet me, and the footman got my luggage from the van. My maid and I went straight to the brougham. I was foolish, perhaps, but I didn't tell anyone what had happened. I dreaded the police knowing. I felt like a thief myself. And—and——"

"You suspected Mr. Kestron, I suppose?"

Her eyes fell before his gaze, and she nodded slowly.

"I don't wonder," said Hazell.

"But—but—do you think he took it, Mr. Hazell? I don't know what to do about it—and my aunt comes home this evening. I shall have to tell her. If—if—he took it, are you going to try to find out?"

"I shall have to keep you in suspense for a little while, Miss Mallaby," said Thorpe Hazell. "I want you to go straight home and say nothing about this visit. Please give me your address, and I will call as soon as possible—to-day, I expect. I can't promise anything, but there is just a chance of getting on the track."

She thanked him. He put on his hat and saw her to the door, where her taxi was waiting. Then he hailed another and directed the driver to take him quickly to the terminus of the West-Northern Railway.

"Wait," he said as he got out. "I shall want you again directly."

He made his way to the office of the traffic-manager, whom he knew.

"I want some information," he said. "Will you tell me if there was a ticket-collector or inspector on the 5.40 p.m. express from Redminster last evening?"

"Another mystery?" asked the official.

"Yes—but the chances are against a solution, I'm afraid."

The manager rang for a clerk and gave some orders. In ten minutes' time the report was brought in. *No ticket inspector or collector had been on the train.*

"That settles it," cried Hazell. "I'd advise you to look after your old uniforms, Mr. Street. Good-morning."

His next move was to drive to Frank Masters, whom he found busy with a pile of briefs in front of him.

"Sorry to disturb you," said Hazell, "but the matter is of importance. It's about your railway journey last night. That ticket-collecting incident is the clue to a mystery. Can you remember what the fellow was like?"

"Yes. A man with a black beard and moustache, and rather a gruff voice."

"After he'd looked at your ticket did he go back along the corridor?"

"No. He passed first, and asked for tickets coming back."

"From the front of the train—yes, I know. Now, whereabouts in the carriage were you—which compartment were you in, I mean?"

"The last but two—a first-class."

"Last but two from the engine?"

"Yes."

"H'm. I wish I knew about those two compartments behind you."

"I can tell you."

"Good!" ejaculated Hazell. "How?"

"There was a fellow in my compartment who lit an Egyptian cigarette. I can't stand the smell of 'em, so I went out."

"After the tickets were looked at?"

"Yes—some ten minutes later—just before we got to Wisden. The next compartment was evidently reserved for ladies, so I avoided it; the last was a second class, but I didn't mind that. There was only one man in it."

"Oh, that's grand," cried Hazell, with great glee. "I'll have a drink on the strength of it."

And he pulled out his milk flask.

"What was he like?" he went on.

"A clean-shaven fellow, with the exception of slight whiskers. He was reading a paper when I went in."

"That's the man I want," said Hazell. "You see, I happen to know that the doors at the ends of the coaches on this train were locked, the key being with the guard. So it was impossible that anyone could get through to the next coach. If only I could find out where that man is now!"

Masters wheeled round his chair suddenly.

"Will you tell me why you want to know?" he asked.

" I can't, my dear chap."

" Will you assure me, then, that no harm will come of it if I can give you a clue ? "

" On the other hand, you will be doing a very great service in the cause of justice."

" Very well, then. I took a taxi straight to the club when I arrived at the terminus. And I happened to notice that my travelling companion took the next on the rank. He had a large Gladstone and a smaller bag with him."

" That settles it. I'm off," exclaimed Hazell.

In half an hour's time he was back at the terminus, in consultation with the cab inspector, who keeps watch at the station gates.

" I want the number and destination of the taxi that followed immediately after the one bound for the Avenue Club last evening—from the 7.35 from Redminster."

He knew, of course, that every cabman has to shout out his destination to the inspector as he passes the little office at the gate. The man consulted his book.

" Number 28,533. Destination, Eight, Lancaster Crescent."

Thorpe Hazell stood as one stunned.

" Kestron's address ! " he muttered to himself. "The girl must have been right, after all. It's pretty bad ! "

" I think you'll find the taxi on the rank now, sir," went on the inspector.

It was there, and in answer to his inquiries the driver informed Hazell that the address was quite correct, and that his fare had certainly gone in at number eight.

" I'm sorry for her," said Hazell to himself, as he

6—Stories of the Railway

told his own cabman to drive him there; "but at least I can try to bluff him. Still, it's very strange. There's a hitch in my reasoning somewhere. Except, of course, this man must have been his tool. *I* can't make it out."

He rang the bell of number eight, and a servant opened the door.

"Is Mr. Kestron in?"

"No, sir; he went out half an hour ago."

Thorpe Hazell paused, then he said:

"Ah, he has returned from the country, then?"

"Yes, sir. He came back late last night."

"About eight?"

"No, sir; not till after ten."

"Oh," said Hazell nonchalantly, "I thought he returned by the train arriving at about half-past seven and drove straight home."

"No, sir; the valet came back with the luggage then, but Mr. Kestron arrived later."

Instantly the solution flashed across his mind. Producing half-a-sovereign, he said to the girl:

"I want to see his valet."

The girl looked at him doubtfully, and hesitated.

"I am a friend of your master," said Hazell quietly.

Then the bribe acted. In a couple of minutes the valet came into the room where Hazell had been shown. Without a word the latter walked to the door and locked it. Then he turned upon the man.

"Do you find ticket-collecting a paying business?" he asked.

The other turned very pale.

"I don't understand," he said.

"I can prove that you were amusing yourself asking for tickets on the express from Redminster last night. I have all the details."

The man was thoroughly taken aback. At first he denied everything, but something in Hazell's quiet manner was too much for him.

"Well," he said sullenly, "and if I was? It was a harmless enough joke. You're from the railway company, I suppose?"

Hazell ignored the question.

"I want that diamond necklace that was handed to you by Miss Mallaby's maid," he said, "sharp!"

The man gave a bound forward.

"It was a clever scheme you both hatched out at Appledon—no!" he cried, "I know exactly what happened. If you attempt any nonsense you're done for, my man." Then he went on to explain that if the necklace were restored quietly nothing more would be said.

"Not for your sake, you know," he added grimly, "but because it's best to hush it up. If you refuse, I'll open the window and tell my cabman to fetch the police. These are my conditions. You give me the necklace, and clear out of here before your master returns. For I fancy *he'll* know about this one of these days."

"Who are you?" blurted out the man.

"My name's Thorpe Hazell—if that's any use to you, and this isn't the first little affair of the railway I've solved."

"I've heard of you," said the valet. "Were you on the train?"

"No. Now then—that necklace, please."

"I'll—I'll go and get it."

"Then I'll come with you."

He looked at Hazell for a moment, then, putting his hand in the inner pocket of his coat he drew out a small case, and handed it over to Hazell with a curse. The latter opened it, and saw the diamonds were intact.

"Thanks," he said. "I've two questions to ask you—out of mere curiosity. Why did you trouble to ask for tickets in every compartment of that carriage?"

"I thought it might allay suspicion if the alarm were given before the end of the journey. The other passengers would——"

"Oh, it is very weak!" interrupted Hazell. "How should you have changed into uniform if there had been anyone else in your compartment?"

"There was the lavatory."

"I see. Good-morning. You may think yourself very lucky, my friend."

In an hour's time the necklace was in the hands of Miss St. John Mallaby, who was profuse in her expressions of relief and gratitude.

"And you are sure that——"

"That Mr. Kestron had nothing to do with it? Absolutely. Now, please ring for your maid."

The latter came in. Hazell held the necklace in his hands.

"Your mistress thinks you had better take yourself off at once," he said. "Mr. Kestron's valet is also out of a situation. Did you use your scissors or a knife to slit open that dressing-case under cover of the rug?"

She stood for half-a-minute gasping for breath. Then she left the room without a word.

"It has been an interesting case, Miss Mallaby," remarked Hazell, "and I am glad to think that the last of my little investigations of railway mysteries has cleared a good man of suspicion and ended happily."

X

THE MYSTERY OF THE BOAT EXPRESS

IT was a gusty, stormy morning in January, with the wind blowing a cold rain from the north-west. There were very few passengers by the Great Southern Boat train to Porthampton that morning, for it was not the day one would choose, if one could help it, for a cross-Channel journey, especially as the telegram from the coast on the station notice-board proclaimed that the Channel was "rough and stormy."

It wanted but three minutes to the starting of the train. A passenger came running from the booking office, a man of about forty years of age, with fair beard and moustache, carrying a small Gladstone bag, a soft hat pulled well down over his eyes, and the collar of his great coat turned up.

"What class, sir?" asked the guard as he drew near.

"Second—please," replied the man.

The guard noticed that he spoke with a slight foreign accent, and opened the door of an empty compartment. The passenger glanced hurriedly along the train, and then got in.

"Will you please lock the door? I do not wish to be disturbed."

The guard took the proffered half-crown, drew a key from his pocket, and turned the lock. The man pulled up the window.

One or two more belated passengers came hurrying to the train—one just as it was about to start. The latter looked hastily into each carriage as he moved along the train.

" Now then, sir—in here, please ! " And the guard opened the door of a compartment, blew his whistle, and the train started.

At Porthampton the guard remembered the locked door, and ran down the platform to release the passenger. He opened the door, and gave a start of surprise.

The occupant of the compartment was huddled up in a heap upon the floor on the further side, his head, with its back to the guard, leaning against the edge of the seat. And staining the cushion of the seat, and the man's shoulder, were splashes of blood.

The guard gave a cry of alarm; a few station officials and passengers pressed forward. One of the latter, an elderly gentleman, exclaimed :

" Then it *was* a shot I heard ! "

" I'll trouble you for your name and address, then, please sir," said a quiet voice. " I am one of the company's detectives."

The other produced his card.

" I am the manager of the City and Southern Bank," he said.

" All right, sir—now let's have a look at the poor chap, and you shall tell us your story later. Someone fetch a doctor."

He went into the compartment, and gently raised the head of the unfortunate man.

"He's dead, I'm afraid—looks as if he shot himself."

"There's a revolver on the seat," exclaimed the guard.

The detective took it up, glanced at it sharply, and put it into his pocket.

"Was he travelling alone?"

"Yes," replied the guard.

"Anyone in the next compartments?"

"This is at the end of the coach. No one was in the next. I'm certain of that."

A doctor came bustling up. They lifted the body on to the seat, and the medical man made an examination.

"A bullet through the brain," he said. "Life must have been extinct for nearly an hour."

"You say you heard a shot, sir?" asked the detective of the bank manager.

"Yes—some time ago. I thought it was a fog signal. I little imagined it meant suicide. Do you want me? I am on my way to Paris, but I shall be back to-morrow."

"You could attend the inquest here if we held it to-morrow evening?"

"Certainly."

The whistle of the steamer sounded, and the little group of passengers hurried away. The detective looked at the doctor, raising his eyebrows.

"Queer, I think, sir?" he asked.

The doctor nodded.

"Half-a-minute," said the other.

He darted out of the carriage.

"Jenkins," he said to a subordinate on the platform, "it's lucky you're here. I want you to board the boat and cross on her. Bring back an account of all the passengers, if you can—there's not a score of them."

" Very good, sir."

The detective went back to the carriage.

" I understand a revolver was found," said the doctor. " Where ? "

The other showed the exact spot on the seat where the weapon had been lying. Then he took it from his pocket and showed it to the doctor. The latter examined it.

" As you say—it's queer," he said. " D'you see what he's got in his right hand ? "

The detective looked.

" A handkerchief ! " he exclaimed. " Will you see about getting the body to the waiting-room, sir ? It may as well lie there. I'll examine the clothes afterwards. I've some work to do here first."

He was a long time in the compartment, and before he left he summoned the guard once more. That night the evening papers had a paragraph stating that an unknown man had apparently committed suicide by shooting himself in the Porthampton boat express. The detective smiled when he read it. His smile changed into a frown, however, when Jenkins returned by the night boat and handed in his report.

" Nothing suspicious about any of them," he said.

" Then he must have slipped off on this side—out of the station," replied his chief enigmatically, " I've bungled it a little."

*   *   *   *   *   *

At the inquest the guard was the first to give evidence. He mentioned that the deceased had spoken to him with a German accent.

" How do you know that? " asked the coroner.

" You can't be guard of the boat train for five years running, sir, without picking up hints. I can generally spot a Frenchman or a German."

He concluded by giving a brief account of his discovery of the body. The coroner asked a few questions, adding :

" No one else could have got in with him? "

" Impossible, sir. The further door was locked already, and, as I said, he asked for the other to be locked."

" He seemed to want to be alone? " asked a juryman.

" Yes."

The juryman nodded sagaciously.

" Suicide—premeditated," he murmured.

Mr. Clinton, the bank manager, was allowed to give evidence next, as he was anxious to catch the last train back to town.

" I was travelling in the compartment next but two to the deceased's," he said, "and was half dozing over a book when I heard a slight report. The wind was very high and both windows were shut."

" A report of a pistol? "

" I didn't think so at the time. There were three other passengers with me, and we all imagined it was probably a detonator on the line, such as is used in fogs or in warning the driver that a gang of men are at work. I am interested in railway matters, and I jumped up at once and looked out of both windows. There was nothing to be seen, and the train did not slacken speed, so we all thought no more about it till I was told at Porthampton what had happened."

" When did you hear the shot? "

" About half an hour after leaving London."

Next came the doctor. He stated, concisely, that death had been caused by a bullet which had entered the deceased's head at the right temple, passed through the skull, and carried away a piece of the bone on the further side. He agreed that the time which had elapsed might reasonably coincide with the shot that Mr. Clinton had heard, and described how he found the body lying on the floor close to the further door."

" As a man might naturally have fallen after he had shot himself?" asked the juryman who had spoken before.

" I don't think so," replied the doctor shortly.

A sensation ran round the court.

" Why not?" asked the coroner.

" There are circumstances in the case which are baffling. The wound was just in the position likely for a man who had shot himself with a pistol, holding it in his right hand with the muzzle against his temple. Death must have been instantaneous. But the strange thing is that the deceased was clutching a handkerchief with his right hand, and that there were no powder marks round the wound. The shot must have been fired at a further distance."

" But," said the coroner, " I understand that a revolver was found in the compartment?"

" It was found before I was on the spot," replied the doctor, " and the next witness will tell you more about it. It is not my professional business," he went on, " to hazard speculation ; but I do say emphatically that, in my opinion, it is certainly not a case of suicide."

The detective corroborated what the doctor had said.

" Tell us about the revolver, please," said the coroner.

" It was lying on the seat—away from the deceased. It was loaded in every chamber, and had not been discharged recently. The barrel was quite clean inside.

" I examined the compartment carefully," he went on, "and although, as the doctor has told you, the bullet went through the skull, carrying away a piece of the bone, I could find neither bone nor bullet—nor any mark of either—in the carriage."

" Was the window open ? " asked a juryman.

" Yes—at the end where the body had fallen. The other was shut. I know what your question implies ; but, if the man had been shot by someone outside the open window, the bullet mark would have been found at the opposite end of the compartment. If, on the other hand, the bullet, after penetrating the skull, had gone out of the open window, the shot must have been fired inside, which appears impossible, especially as both doors were found locked ; and the murderer could not have opened the other window from outside and then fired through it."

" What is your opinion, then ? " asked the coroner.

" Murder," he replied, " but *how* I cannot say."

" You have taken steps ? "

" As far as is possible."

He stated further that there was no clue to identify the dead man. He carried no papers, his bag only contained clothing, and his linen was not marked."

" Nothing else ? "

The witness hesitated.

" There was something which *might* be a possible

clue, sir; but I will ask you not to make me mention it—at present."

An adjournment was made for a fortnight at the request of the police. But at the adjournment the detective said bluntly that he had no more evidence, and the inspector of police who was in charge of the case was equally reticent.

Finally, the jury returned the rather strange verdict of "Found shot—apparently by some person unknown," and the newspapers curtly referred to the case as "another unsolved railway mystery."

*   *   *   *   *   *

So much for the story. I had the sequel from the very man who unravelled the mystery, now retired from business on a comfortable pension. He was telling me some of his exploits one day, when I happened to mention the Porthampton Murder.

"That was a curious affair," I said. "You never solved it, did you?"

He filled and lit his pipe thoughtfully.

"I can't say I didn't do *that*," he replied; "but" —and he laughed—"I wasn't allowed to get the credit of it. The official police stopped me. Look here," he went on, "it happened five years ago, and is forgotten; I don't mind telling you the tale, if you like."

"I'd better begin at the start," he continued. "I was pretty convinced from the first that the murderer—if there were one—had been on the train, and probably given us the slip at Porthampton Station. But I had very little to go upon. As a sort of forlorn hope, however, it dawned upon me that something might be discovered if I found the exact spot on the line where the bank manager—Mr. Clinton—had heard the shot. He had said it was

about half an hour after leaving London. I ran up
to town the morning after the inquest, and called on
him.

"' Can't you recollect exactly *where* it was on the
line ? ' I asked.

" He thought for a minute.

"' Let me see—yes, I can. We ran through
Hazleton Station a minute or so afterwards.'

"' Hazleton ; ' I exclaimed. 'A big village, I
think ? Now, Mr. Clinton, when you looked out,
you're *sure* you saw no one—on the footboard, for
example ? '

"' Positive. I couldn't have helped seeing anyone if he had been there. I glanced both up and
down the track on both sides.'

" I took the next train to Hazleton, determined
to patrol the line for a mile or so up from the
station. It was just a remote possibility that I
might find something—perhaps, even, a pistol!

" It was a fruitless search, however. So, giving
it up, I made up my mind to seek a place of refreshment. A road ran parallel with the up side of the
line, quite close. I climbed over the palings for
easier walking, and got into the road. There were
a few small houses, almost new, of the suburban
villa type, for Hazleton was getting a name as a
picturesque neighbourhood, being only half-an-hour's
run from town.

" As I walked along, thinking that the train must
have been passing close by the spot when the mysterious tragedy happened, my glance fell on the gate-
post of one of the villas. On it was the name of the
house, ' The Maples.'

" I gave a start, and I'll tell you why. You may
remember that at the inquest I stated there was a

small, possible clue, which I wished to keep to myself. In the pocket of the murdered man I had found a current number of a newspaper, on the outside cover of which was scrawled in pencil those very words—'The Maples.'

"At once I made up my mind. I found my way to the only newspaper shop in the village, and made some inquiries. At what hour could I have a morning paper delivered? I was told the newspaper train arrived pretty early, and that the boy started on his rounds at seven. I chatted away, leading the conversation up to ' The Maples.' Yes, they sent papers to that house.

" ' Who lives there? ' I asked casually.

" ' Foreigners, I think, sir. They haven't been long at Hazleton. I've quite forgotten their name for the moment.'

"I was evidently on a track. Sometimes boldness is the best action for discovering things, so I determined to call at ' The Maples.' The point was this: The paper found on the man had evidently been left at this house the very morning he was murdered. The obvious deduction was that the poor wretch himself had been in the house.

"The door was opened by a fair-haired young woman, with a pale, anxious face. I saw, at a glance, she had been crying.

" ' What is it, please, you want? ' she asked nervously, with a strong foreign accent.

"I came to the point at once.

" ' Information about a fellow-countryman of yours who left this house early on Tuesday morning and was found dead in the Porthampton boat express,' I said.

She clasped her hands together, and gave a little cry.

"'*Ach !*' she exclaimed, 'are you of the *English* police ?'

"'Not exactly,' I replied, 'I am in the service of the railway company.'

"She hesitated. I thought she was about to faint. Then, pulling herself together with an effort, she said :

"'Will you come in? You need not fear—there is no one else in the house.'

"She led me into a sitting-room, sat down, wringing her hands, and said, in a low voice :

"'He was my brother!'

"'Your brother? But if you knew—why have you not identified him ?'

"She shook her head.

"'I was afraid—they might kill me, too—*Himmel* —but you do not know how I am suffering.'

"'Then you know he was murdered ?' I asked in surprise.

"She nodded.

"'I saw it,' she gasped, 'it has haunted me ever since—it was terrible—and I could do nothing. Poor André!'

"'Come,' I said, 'you must tell me everything. I want to be your friend.'

"'But—but,' she faltered, 'it is the police whom I fear—and the others. You do not know.'

"'My dear young lady,' I said, 'I assure you you have nothing to fear from the police. They are only too anxious to find the murderer. And, if you know, you can help them.'

"She shook her head again.

"'You do not understand,' she said. There was a long pause. Then she spoke again, more calmly :

"'I will tell you,' she said. 'Since you have

discovered so much, I was afraid of this.   My name is Cambon.   André and I are natives of Alsace, of French extraction, but of German nationality.   And, you see, we were both in the Secret Service of the German Government.   I cannot tell you how it all happened, but Herr Otto Schuster had us in his hands—he is a bad man.   It began by accident ; a little sketch that I made of one of your English forts, and André mentioned it.   Schuster paid us for it ; we were poor, and ever since he has held us in his hand.'

" ' There is a retired officer of your artillery living here in Hazleton, Major Dent.   He had invented a new gun, and your War Office was going to make experiments with it.   Schuster told us we must come down here and try and get the drawings, so he took this house for us.   We got to know the Major—I taught his little girl German, and—well I got hold of the plans and made a rough copy.'

" ' And sold it to Schuster ? '

" ' No.   That is why it all happened.   It was Pierre Duprez who interfered.   You do not know him ?   Oh, he is one of the cleverest spies of the French Government, and he found out what we were doing.   He came here and saw my brother, just as we were about to send the plans to Schuster.   He appealed to André's French parentage—he entreated —reviled him for being a false Alsatian—for many of us still hate the Germans, though we obey them. And André gave way.   He gave the plans to Pierre Duprez, and Duprez was to pay him twenty thousand francs—to his order at a bank in Paris.   We meant to retire then—to get away from the power of Otto Schuster.   That was last Monday, and Duprez took the plans back with him to London.

"'It was early on Tuesday morning that the warning came, by the first post. Pierre Duprez sent it. He said that Schuster had found out, and advised my brother to go to Paris at once. There was scarcely time to arrange anything, for André saw that he must take the next train to town to catch the boat express. I packed up a few things in his bag, and he put in his revolver. He was very nervous and afraid of Schuster, and said he should keep the weapon ready during the whole journey. I was to follow him in a few days' time. Then we arranged a signal, so that I should know he had caught the express. He was to wave his handkerchief from the window as the train passed this house.

"'Can you guess now? Schuster must have tracked him to the train, but was too late to get in with him. I stood just outside the front door, waiting. Then the train came in sight, and I saw André leaning out of the window, waving his handkerchief. I waved mine in return. Schuster must have seen me doing so, and that evidently gave him the idea that André was leaning out of the carriage, and that an unexpected chance of killing him had offered itself.

"'For, suddenly, just as the train was opposite the house, I saw a man's head and arm come out of a window two compartments behind my brother. Something shone in his hand; he leant forward, took aim at André, there was a flash, and I saw my brother fall back into the carriage, while Schuster, for it was near enough to recognise him, immediately retired into his.'

"Now I understood why no traces of bone or bullet were found. The latter went through Cambon's head while it was outside the carriage.

" Well, by strong arguments, I prevailed upon his sister to go to town with me at once. Now she had told her story a new idea seemed to have got possession of her. The phase of fright was passing. Vengeance was taking its place.

" 'Yes, I will go with you,' she said, ' I don't care what your police do with me—if they find Otto Schuster.'

" But I had my doubts and said nothing. It was as I had expected. The Chief Inspector at Scotland Yard took down the information without comment, thought for a few minutes, and then said :

" ' I will ask you to stay here a short time, I am going to the Foreign Office. This is a very peculiar matter, and I cannot handle it without advice.'

" In an hour's time he was back. A grim smile was on his face. He turned to Fräulein Cambon.

" ' It may be some satisfaction to you to know that any charge against you for purloining valuable secrets has fallen through. Major Dent is not so artless as you supposed. His drawings were under lock and key at the War Office.'

" ' But— ! ' she began, in astonishment.

" ' What you copied were old designs, of no value,' he interrupted drily, ' as M. Duprez will doubtless discover before long.'

" She sprang from her seat.

" ' So ! ' she cried, ' André has been murdered for nothing ! But you will find this Schuster—ah, you English police are so clever ! You will hang him, yes—— '

" The Chief waved his hand.

" ' Madam,' he said, ' my instructions are simply

to see that you leave the country at once. With the rest we have nothing to do. When one enters the Secret Service of a Government one takes all risks, and you and your brother ought to have known this. You will understand,' he went on, turning to me, 'that nothing is to be done by us, and that *you* are to proceed no further.'

"'You will not find Schuster. You will not avenge my poor brother?" she shrieked.

" He shook his head.

"'Then,' she said, in a low voice, 'I will avenge André myself. I will never rest until—— '

"The Chief cut her short. He evidently had little sympathy with spies.

"'You may do what you please, madam, but I warn you that it must not be in this country.'

"Whether she carried out her threat or not I often wonder. At all events Otto Schuster, the German Secret Service agent, was found stabbed in the back in one of the narrow streets of Genoa not a year afterwards, and I have sometimes thought it may have been the sequel to the Porthampton boat express mystery."

XI

HOW THE EXPRESS WAS SAVED

THE strike on the Mid-Northern Railway was not very prominent in the public eye. The daily papers, full of a murder sensation, had devoted only small paragraphs to it — paragraphs which had been relentlessly slaughtered with blue pencil before they left the sub-editors' room. Passengers on the railway noticed nothing at all. Trains still ran fairly up to the scheduled time, guards and porters took tips as usual. Nothing seemed amiss to the casual eye.

The reason was that only one section of the great army of workers of the Mid-Northern Railway had laid down their arms, or rather their tools, and these particular tools were shovels and pickaxes, and crowbars and spanners. It was a platelayers' strike— based on a shilling a week extra and an obdurate board of directors.

In this particular instance the officials considered the strike was unjustified, a breach of certain contracts made in a recent conciliation, and they had taken the strong line of not only refusing to discuss the men's demands, but also of giving it out that certain of the ringleaders need not trouble to return to work at all. The strike was by no means general; a certain proportion of employees remained on duty, and no trouble had been encountered in obtaining the services of a few hundreds of " out of works."

A dozen men were gathered together in the stuffy little bar of the " Red Lion " at Hillingdon. At all times you would have expected the railway element to predominate in that particular bar, for Hillingdon was a big junction on the Mid-Northern and the " Red Lion " stood in the very centre of a district, nine-tenths of the inhabitants of which were employed in the Company's service.

The subject of discussion was, naturally, the platelayers' strike.

" Well, there ain't much wrong with the road," remarked the fireman of a goods engine. " Everything up to time. You wouldn't know anything was up at all."

" It's those blacklegs that are upsetting things," replied a thick-set man with a scowling face who lounged in a corner. " If it wasn't for them takin' on our job you wouldn't ha' had such an easy run down."

The fireman laughed. He was young and cheeky.

" They'll want someone to take on *your* job for good and all, Yates," he said, "from what I hear."

Joe Yates darted an angry look at him and replied with an oath. He was one of the men whom the Company had refused to take back, he and another named Ford being the ringleaders of discontent at Hillingdon.

" Steady on, Tom," growled one of the men to the fireman, "your tongue's too loose, my lad."

" Got many chaps at work up the line ? " asked another platelayer.

The fireman nodded.

" Yes—a lot. You haven't even stopped 'em

putting down the new rails 't'other side o' Cranbury. There's a good forty of 'em there—hard at it."

"Ought to be shot," muttered Joe Yates, "what business have they to take the bread out 'o the mouths o' us, eh?"

The fireman drained his glass, and replaced it on the counter.

"Might as well ask what business have you chaps to take the bread out o' the mouths o' your wives and children," he answered as he went to the door.

With another oath Joe Yates sprang forward. A few hands were stretched out to stop him, but he had almost gained the door when a newcomer entered and barred the way—a tall, sinewy man in corduroys.

"Chuck it, Joe," he exclaimed. "If it's that young fool of a Stimson you're after he ain't worth wastin' muscle on. Come and have a drink with me."

It was Harry Ford himself. By mutual consent the others dropped the subject of the strike while the two men drank sullenly and in silence. Presently Ford said to the other:

"Coming out?"

"Don't mind if I do."

"Come on then. Good-night, all."

It was raining steadily, and very dark. The two men walked slowly along the street, and then Ford led the way to a waste, unfrequented bit of ground.

"Look here," he remarked suddenly, "it's not much of a look-out for you and me, is it Joe?"

"That it ain't—curse 'em!" replied the other.

"Curse 'em by all means, but *that* won't do 'em no harm. Ain't you game for something more?"

"What d'ye mean, Harry?"

"I heard a bit o' news just now. The G.M.'s*
coming down to Hillingdon to-night—by the express
that gets here at 11.53."

"Well, what o' that?"

Ford's voice sank to a low whisper.

"Well, supposing that train was to run off the
metals just afore it got to Buckley Bridge."

"Eh?"

"I say, supposing a length o' rail was taken out
just t'other side o' the bridge—chance for the whole
train and the G.M. in it to pitch into the river, eh?"

"What are you driving at, Harry?" asked Joe
Yates, sinking his voice to a whisper.

"A spanner and a hammer 'ud soon do it,"
replied the other, "and the night's made for it."

"But—if we were seen?"

"Look here, Joe. How far off is Buckley
Bridge?"

"Matter o' four miles up the line."

"Then if we were seen here in Hillingdon at a
quarter to eleven no one 'ud even suspect us o' the
job, eh?"

"But how would we get there in time?"

"The 10.55 goods to Wharnton. Leaves No. 5
siding. We could easily get into a truck. And she
has to slow down at Buckley signal box to get the
staff for the Wharnton branch. We could drop off
there and be right on the job. Are you game for it?"

"Done!"

"Right. You show yourself in the "Red Lion"
later on; I'll go to some other pub. Meet me
alongside the goods just before 10.55. She'll be

General Manager.

marshalled ready for starting.   And bring a spanner.
I'll get hold of a crow-bar."

*   *   *   *   *   *

Buckley Bridge, or "Bridge No. 74," as it was
technically called, was an iron bridge, of some fifty
yards in length, spanning the river, some four miles
away from Hillingdon on the up line.   It was used
for the service of trains only, and was guarded by a
light iron railing on either side.

A little way on the Hillingdon side of the
bridge stood a signal box.   This box guarded
the junction where the single branch line to
Wharnton struck off from the main line.   The
customary signals were placed to protect this
junction, of which two only need be described in
the present narrative.   These were the "distant"
and the "home" signals which warned approaching
trains on the down main line, and they were both
on the side of the bridge farthest away from the
signal box.

The "distant" signal was half-a-mile up the line,
the "home" signal about a hundred yards before
the bridge.   There was, therefore, ample protection
for the down trains, as if the junction or the block
beyond it on the Hillingdon side were not clear the
train would be brought to a stop well before it
reached the bridge.

Beyond the bridge, where the main line ran on to
the signal box, it curved slightly to the right, so that
the man on duty could not actually see the down
home signal.   But, by means of that wonderful little
instrument, the electric repeater, he could tell
its position exactly, the miniature semaphore arm in
the little glass case in front of him imitating every

movement of the signal itself as he pulled or replaced
the lever.

In the signal box were
two men, the signalman
on duty and a young
linesman. It was the
duty of the latter to
patrol a certain length
of the road with a view
to inspecting and repair-
ing electric and signal-
ling apparatus. Some
trifling defect had been
found that evening in
the interlocking gear
beneath the Buckley
box, and Charles Palmer
had been working at it
overtime. He had now
come up from the net-
work of bars and wires
below the box, and was
smoking his pipe in the
cabin.

He was packing up
his tools as he smoked.
One or two, such as his
folding rule and a small
pair of wire cutters, he
put in his pocket from
force of habit. The
rest he arranged in his
bag.

A ring came at the bell.

"The Wharnton Goods," said the signalman, as

he returned the answer and pulled the levers that "took off" the up main home and distant signals.

"You'll be wanting the staff for her," said Palmer.

"That's right."

He went up to the curious-looking electric machine that held the staves for the Wharnton Branch, signalled forward to the block ahead on the single line, obtained, by means of electric release, a long brass staff from the machine, and then threw open his window and peered down the line. Two flickering lights, a green above a white, showed that the goods train was approaching. The engine came to a standstill just beside the box, and the signalman ran down the steps and handed the staff to the driver.

"A rough night, Bill."

"No mistake," replied the driver, as he opened the throttle valve. "Good-night, mate!"

Out of a low truck midway along the goods train Yates and Ford dropped stealthily to the ground on the side farther from the signal box, climbed the fence bordering the line, and, stooping down, hurried along parallel with the track through fields until they came to the bank of the river. Here they turned aside, reclimbed the fence, and passed over the iron bridge.

"Got your spanner, Joe?" asked Ford, in a low voice.

"All right."

"There's not too much time—we shall have to look sharp."

"Can't start till the local's gone by."

"Ah, I forgot that. Hullo—there's the signal for her."

"Crash!" went the arm of the down home signal which stood about a hundred yards beyond them. The two men hid themselves as the local train came by, and then sprang on to the track.

"Here you are," said Ford, "we'll soon have it out. I only helped to put it in three weeks ago," he added, with a grim chuckle. "You take that end, I'll tackle this."

Rails are secured to each other at the ends by flat pieces of metal known as "fish plates," to which they are fixed by bolts. The object of the two men was to remove one of the rails immediately in front of the bridge, rightly calculating that if the engine ran off at that point the train would probably be wrecked in the river.

It was work to which they were well accustomed, and accustomed to do it smartly as well. As a rule old rails are replaced by new ones without in any way interfering with the running of the trains, and over and over again the passenger little dreams as he runs along securely that a new rail was inserted only a few minutes before.

With their stout, curved spanners, they loosened and unscrewed the nuts which fastened the bolts holding the two fish plates to the rails. In a very short time the fish plates themselves were off and lying alongside the line. Then came the knocking out of the wooden "keys" which held the rail in the "chairs" fixed down to the sleepers. They looked round once or twice, for they could not loosen the keys without a slight noise of hammering, but the wind was rising, drowning all sounds. Then the rail lay loose.

Next came the supreme effort. Long rails weighing 106 lb. to the yard take some moving. Both men were strong, but it wanted all their strength put forth before the rail was lifted out of the chairs and fell with a muffled clang at the side of the line.

Then the unexpected happened. Charles Palmer had started for his home, and his home was in a village the further side of the river from the signal box. There was a road bridge two miles away; there was the convenient railway bridge close at hand. And he, naturally, chose the nearer route. The sky was clearing a little, a waning moon had risen and was showing a pale light through the rain-clouds. Half-way over the bridge he fancied he saw something moving; just as he was over there came the clang of the metal, and when Yates and Ford looked up he was there—right upon them—with his fists clenched.

"You scoundrels!" he cried, as he rushed forward.

Ford, however, was perfectly cool. His brawny arm went out straight from the shoulder, and his fist caught Palmer right on the chin. The young man went down like a log.

"Curse him!" cried Ford beneath his breath, "look sharp, Yates. There's no time to lose. Got any cord or anything?"

"Here's a bit o' stout twine."

"Tie his legs together—ah, would you!" he exclaimed as Palmer made an attempt to cry out. "I'll stuff something in his mouth and tie it in with a handkerchief—we must fix his arms, too. I know —good, he's got leather laces in his boots—that's better than cord."

In five minutes Charles Palmer lay beside the line gagged, his feet tied together and his hands cruelly fastened behind him with his own bootlaces, while Ford and Yates had gained the further side of the river and were hurrying back to Hillingdon along unfrequented by-roads.

They paused once for breath.

"He'll be smashed up," whispered Yates, thinking of Palmer.

"Let him be!" replied the other savagely, "if he isn't we'll have to make tracks—for I believe he recognised us."

*   ⁂   *   *   *   *

Charles Palmer lay for a few minutes half dazed. Then he began to realise not only his own terrible position, but the fact of the gaping void between the line of rail. Nothing could save the express from being wrecked. It was, he knew almost due now.

"Twang—crash!" the sounds came simultaneously. The down home signal was pulled off. He glanced at the place where the post should be. Yes—the extinguishing disc had passed over the white "back light," so that green showed on the other side.

"Twang!" That was for the distant signal. The train was on the block now, and the line was signalled "clear."

And then a desperate thought, arising from a pain in his thigh, came into his mind. If only he could do it! Writhing and twisting he wriggled himself slowly away from the metals to the side of the line. His face touched something cold. Good! It was what he was seeking for—the wire that communicated with the home signal.

A great effort, and he lay with his back to the wire. Could he do it? With extreme difficulty and with the laces cutting into his flesh he managed to get a couple of fingers into his hip pocket, felt for the cutters, drew them slowly out, held them in his hand, and groped for the wire behind him.

The weighted safety lever at the base of the home signal, relieved of the tension of the wire, fell, resetting the semaphore arm at "danger," and showing the red light.

A whistle, the grinding of brakes, a shower of sparks along the wheels, and the great express came to a standstill.

What was up? In the signal box the man knew something had given way. The tell-tale repeater stood at "line blocked." The engine whistle clamoured for a clear road. The road *was* clear. Seizing a lantern he came down from the signal box and ran along the line, past the curve, till he could see the back light.

He waved the lantern for the train to advance slowly, running forward over the bridge as he did so.

Then, with a shout, he turned on the red glass of his lantern and waved it frantically. He had seen the gap in the metals—and the man beside the line. The train was saved !

And to-day Charles Palmer holds a prominent position in the electrical and engineering department of the Mid-Northern.

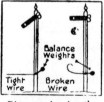

Diagram showing the mechanism of the balance weights and signals.

XII

A CASE OF SIGNALLING

THE 2.15 goods train moved slowly out of No. 14 siding at the big terminal station of Sterrington on the Great Southern Railway, and commenced its ponderous journey on the main up line. To railway men the train was ironically known as the "after-noon flier," a name given to it in scorn and derision. All the way along the line it stopped at every station to pick up empties, and was shunted into every refuge siding in between stations to make way for its betters.

Finally, it accomplished the seventy or eighty odd miles of its journey in something under seven hours, more or less. It was rumoured that at more than one point the brakesman had his regular nap while the driver and fireman comfortably read stray newspapers in their cab.

Along the route they were subjected to mild chaff from porters on platforms or signalmen who hauled them up. "Broken the record to-day, Jim?" "Been racing a funeral?" "What sort o' weather did you leave at Sterrington last week?" These, and similar observations, broke upon the ear of old Jim Harvey, but without the slightest impression.

On the return journey at night he made up for it. He backed his engine on to a "fast mineral" train that came pounding down at twenty or thirty miles an hour, with only three stops to take off loaded trucks until she was held up in Fairdale refuge siding three miles out of Sterrington for fifteen or twenty minutes, to allow of the passing of the night passenger down express.

Jim Harvey stood on the footplate of his dingy, but powerful goods engine, "notching her up" slightly as she took the road and gained in speed, his eyes fixed on the signals in the distance. His grey head turned occasionally to observe the manner in which George Ledbury, his young fireman, put on coal—a task calling for the exercise of more skill than the outsider is aware of.

George Ledbury was a new mate, having only recently been promoted from the footplate of an insignificant "local goods" to work on the main line. He had great visions of the day when he should drive a crack express train like the one that came snorting past them on the down road.

"That'll do," said the driver with a grunt of approbation; "she won't want any more before she gets to the Belton rise."

The fireman put down his short shovel, gave the footplate a brush round, wiped his hands on a bit of waste, and took his place on the other side of the cab. He was a good-looking young man, in spite of the fact that at this particular moment he had a big smudge on one of his cheeks. He gave one the idea of being quick and alert, and there was a twinkle in his blue eyes that spoke of happiness.

They were passing through the suburbs of the large town of Sterrington now, and the streets of small houses had given place to broad avenues with large villas of a superior class. This suburb of

Fairdale was noted for its quiet and beauty. Many
of the wealthy manufacturers and business men had
their houses there, together with a sprinkling of the
"retired."

The country began to open out, and fields appeared.
About three hundred yards from the line were some
half-a-dozen good-sized detached houses standing in
their own grounds with their backs to the railway—
almost the last houses of the suburb. The fireman's
gaze shifted from the signals ahead to one of these
houses; he drew a clean-white handkerchief from
his pocket, and, turning his back to the driver,
suddenly began waving it to and fro with peculiar
motion.

Jim Harvey, glancing over his shoulder across
the cab, suddenly caught sight of these mysterious
movements. He was about to speak, when, looking
beyond over the field, he saw something else which
brought a grin over his weather-beaten face.

Standing at an open window at the back of one of
the aforesaid houses a female figure in a white apron
could just be discerned, and there came the answering waving of a handkerchief.

"Is she a pretty girl, George?"

George Ledbury turned round, stuffed the handkerchief into his pocket, and the smudge on his face
showed upon a crimson background.

"Ask me to the wedding when it comes off, won't
you, mate?"

George laughed uneasily.

"All right," he said, "there's nothing to be
ashamed of."

"Not a bit, my lad," replied the old driver cheer-
ily. "I've been through it myself and I wish you
luck. Got a place over there?"

And he jerked his thumb in the direction of the house.

"Yes.   She's a parlourmaid to a fussy old retired major and his wife."

"You were waving your handkerchief in a funny way—and so was she," went on the driver.

"Morse code," replied the fireman.

"What do you mean?"

"Before I was in the sheds, I was in a signal-box for a year and learnt the code.   I've been teaching it to Maggie."

"Oho!" exclaimed Jim Harvey, "signalling, eh? What was it you said?"

The young man blushed crimson again and looked uncomfortable.

"*Best love*," he blurted out.

The other laughed heartily.

"And what did she say?"

"Oh—something—something about a kiss—only she didn't spell it quite right.   She hasn't quite got hold of the code yet."

"Well I'm blowed!" said the driver.   "Hullo— bit o' stick against us.   Brakes, George!"

A "bit o' stick" in the shape of a semaphore arm at right angles to the post faced them.   The driver shut off steam, the fireman screwed down the hand brake.

*   *   *   *   •   *

George Ledbury had each second Sunday off. Maggie Bond's alternate Sunday afternoon out, strangely enough, coincided with it.   Therefore it came to pass that the following Sunday they might have been seen in the country outside Fairdale walking arm in arm.   Only, instead of his dirty

dungaree overalls, George wore a well-fitting dark
blue serge suit, had a face that was clean enough
for the occasional kiss he got in return for a dozen
given, and looked, in every way, an exceedingly
spruce young man. The conversation need not be
recorded, being of the " As it was and ever shall be,
world without end " description.

"What's the time, George?" Maggie asked
presently.

"Five forty-seven," he replied, in true railway
parlance, after glancing at his watch.

" That's ten minutes to six," she exclaimed, with
a woman's usual comprehension of exact figures,
"and if I'm not back by six there'll be an awful
row. The master is just about irritable if you're
not back exactly in time."

" Bother the master," replied George, " we'd best
be getting back, then."

It struck six before they reached the house. Outside the gate he demanded a farewell kiss, got it,
and gave three in exchange, the entire performance
being observed, unknown to the actors therein, by
Major Blake, who was strolling round his garden.

Off went George Ledbury, walking with head
erect and heart aglow down Sinclair Avenue—the
name of the quiet little street—and in through the
gate went Maggie, to be confronted by the stern
little Major.

" Margaret, you're ten minutes late."

" Very sorry, sir."

" Who was that young man you were kissing?"
Maggie blushed violently.

"He's—he's a friend, sir."

" Margaret, I'm ashamed of you."

She drew herself up a little.

" We're engaged to be married, sir," she said a trifle defiantly.

"Oh, *are* you! Why, you're not out of your teens. Understand me, Margaret, that I won't have any followers about my house. I object to it. Who is he?"

"A fireman on the railway, sir."

"Oh! One of those fellows who are always going on strike; a lazy lot. You'd better have nothing more to do with him. Anyhow, don't let *me* catch him about my house. Go indoors at once. Your mistress wants you."

He spoke as one addressing a private in a regiment, and started for a walk, very satisfied with himself. He did not notice two well-dressed men who were strolling along Sinclair Avenue, although they, apparently, eyed him with interest. He might have seen one of them the next day talking casually to his gardener at the dinner hour, and eliciting certain information about himself.

He returned from his walk and found his wife in the drawing-room. She was a weak little woman. But then she had been married five-and-twenty years to Major Blake.

" I've had to give Margaret a lecture, my dear," he began. " The girl has a sweetheart."

" Oh, I know," she replied, " Margaret has just given me a month's notice."

Major Blake's periodical "lectures" to the domestics meant a constant source of worry to Mrs. Blake and an increase of fees to the local registry office for servants.

" Impudent hussy! " exclaimed the Major, " we're well rid of her."

His wife sighed.

"I'm sorry she's going, dear. She's been a very good servant—and they are not easy to get."

"Pooh!" rejoined the Major. "I won't have men coming about my house. I'd rather be without servants altogether. ·I don't want to be robbed."

Later on that evening he smoked his cigar and sipped his whiskey and water in a little room he called his "study," but which was not blessed with many books. In one corner was a large iron safe. The Major was a collector, and a collector with expensive tastes. That safe contained a variety of precious stones, chiefly uncut.

He opened it, glancing with a collector's pride at the contents, which were arranged in various trays. It was his silver wedding day soon, and he was going to give his wife a necklace made from uncut Indian sapphires. He picked out about a dozen of the pale blue stones.

"These will do very well," he said to himself, "I can take them up to town with me when we go on Tuesday. By the way, I must go and talk over trains with Kate."

It was on the following Tuesday afternoon that Major Blake and his wife went to London. He had a parting shot at Maggie Bond as he was going out of the house.

"Now, Margaret," he said, "remember what I told you. I won't have that young fellow about my premises while I'm away."

The little servant tossed her head. She was not over particular in her reply.

"Very well, sir. I'll leave myself now if you don't think——"

"Nonsense, Margaret," broke in Mrs. Blake.

"We shall be back Thursday morning. See that the fire is lighted in your master's study."

So it came to pass that Maggie was left alone with the cook. The latter was slightly deaf and fond of reading penny novelettes, so Maggie was left much to her own resources. She waved her handkerchief as usual to George Ledbury as his train passed on the Wednesday afternoon.

At ten o'clock that evening she accompanied the cook, who was a trifle nervous, round the house to lock up. Then both servants went to bed, the cook sleeping in an attic in front of the house and Maggie occupying a similar room at the back.

It was about one a.m., and unusually dark, when two men came stealthily down Sinclair Avenue, each of them carrying a large black bag. Arrived at Major Blake's house they entered the gate, crossed the lawn on tip-toe, and proceeded to a window at the side of the building.

Then, with the help of a glazier's diamond and a circular bit of leather soaked in water, they quickly and skilfully removed half a pane of glass. The rest was easy, and in five minutes' time they were bending over the safe in the Major's study on the second floor, examining it with a small electric lantern.

"A good two hours' work," whispered one of them.

"Let's get at it, then. Out with the tools."

It may be that they made a slight noise in opening their bags and arranging their tools. At any rate, Maggie awoke with a start and listened attentively. She was by no means a nervous girl, and, somehow, the fear or even the thought of burglars never entered her head. What was really agitating her mind was the problem as to whether she had shut the window in her master's study. She remembered opening it in the morning, but she could not recollect whether she had closed it with the other windows in the afternoon. A slight wind was rising. She got out of bed, opened the door, and listened.

A gentle "swishing" sound came from below, just such a sound as the wind blowing about the curtain in a room might make. She determined to be certain. Throwing on a skirt and jacket, after having lighted a candle, she went downstairs quietly, so as not to awaken the cook, and threw open the door of the study.

Two men were on their knees in front of the safe. Before she could recover from her surprise or utter a cry they were upon her, and she felt a strong hand pressed over her mouth.

"All right, my dear," whispered one of them, "don't be frightened. We won't hurt you. But we'll have to keep you quiet. Joe—your handkerchief—that's right—sorry to deprive you of your voice, miss."

"Is it safe?" whispered the other.

"Safe as nails. There's only the cook in the house beside her, and she's deaf. We won't run for this. But we must tie her up."

The gardener had been pumped effectively.

In one of their bags was a bit of rope. The girl struggled, but they tied her feet together.

"Let's take her into the bedroom—next door, Joe."

This was Major and Mrs. Blake's room. They laid Maggie on the bed, drew one of her arms through the brasswork at the head of the bedstead, and tied her wrists together.

"Sorry if it's a bit uncomfortable, my dear," said the first man, "but it can't be helped. Cook'll find you all right in the morning—here, you mustn't catch cold!"

He threw the eiderdown over her, and the two men left the room, locking the door on the outside cautiously.

"Come along, Joe, we've got to get this safe open —and it's worth it."

Maggie lay on the bed, bound and gagged. But the tight cords round her wrists and ankles did not hurt her half so much as the thought that she was to blame. For she felt sure the burglars had entered through the window which she believed, wrongly, she had left open.

It made her nearly mad to think of her employers being robbed while she was helpless to do anything. She did not quite know what was in the safe, except that certain valuables were kept there. What could she do? If only cook would wake! But, if she did, she would probably lock herself in her bedroom from fear, and the thieves would get off. *If* she could give the alarm!

She turned and twisted in a vain endeavour to free herself, but, as she did so, one of her hands came in contact with something against the wall by the head of the bed. It was the button of the electric light. She twisted it, and the room was illuminated instantly by a lamp hanging from the centre of the ceiling. Just then the clock on the mantelpiece struck two. An idea suddenly occurred to her. She turned off the light and thought it out —trying to remember certain things. The window was at the back of the house, and, fortunately, she had not troubled to draw down the blind.

For a quarter of an hour she lay waiting—waiting —listening to every tick of the clock. She heard a train go by. That was the up "fish special." It could not be long now. No! There came a series of sonorous puffs, suddenly ceasing, and then, "bang—bang—bang" as the brakes of the down goods engine were put on and the buffers of the heavily-laden trucks behind came crashing together.

A whistle—then more puffs—and she knew that the train was being shunted back into the refuge siding just opposite the house, where it would remain till the up express passed. And George Ledbury was on the footplate of that stationary engine. If only he would look that way! With this prayer on her gagged lips, she felt again for the little electric button.

     ❖   ❖   ❖   ❖   *   *

Driver Harvey filled his pipe, struck a match and lighted it. He was looking forward to the end of his run and the comfortable bed awaiting him. He folded his arms and leant against the side of the cab meditatively.

Suddenly he exclaimed:

"Hullo! Does that girl of yours try to talk to you in the middle of the night?"

George Ledbury was down by the side of the engine with a lamp and an oilcan.

"What's up?" he asked.

The driver pointed to the dark outline of the houses in the near distance.

"Look there," he said, "that's your girl's place, ain't it? What's she up to? Blowing you kisses when she ought to be in bed and asleep? I'm ashamed of her!"

And he gave a quiet chuckle.

But George's gaze was fixed on a certain window. Flashes of light were coming from it in irregular succession, some of them momentary, others prolonged. He recognised the Morse code in a second.

"What's she saying?" asked the driver, with another chuckle.

The fireman sprang on the footplate.

"Two words—over and over again—this is the third time."

"What are they, mate?"

"'*Help—Whistle!*'" exclaimed the other, reaching for a little handle at the top of the fire-box.

"What are you up to?" cried the driver.

But George gave no heed to him. A series of shrill screams rose in the night. He was signalling back with the whistle—just two words.

"*What's up?*"

Then he waited, his eyes fixed on the distant window. Back came the flashes of light.

"Well?" asked the driver.

"'*Thieves—in—the—house—help*,'" exclaimed George Ledbury, as he made out each word. At this moment the express came thundering by.

"I must go," cried George.

The driver put a heavy hand on his shoulder.

"No, my lad," he said, quietly, "you mustn't leave your duty. Besides, I've a better notion than that. Whistle back '*Help coming soon*,' will you? Ah, the signal's off. Go on whistling, mate."

He opened the regulator and the train moved slowly forward, the whistle screeching out its message. Opposite the signal-box he pulled up. The man on duty had his head out of the window.

"What's the matter?" he shouted. "What's all this row about help coming?"

For, of course, he understood the code.

"All right," sang out the driver, "there's burglars in one o' those houses yonder. Tell him which, George."

"Major Blake's house—'Alma,' Sinclair Avenue."

"You telephone on to Sterrington and ask 'em to send the police out—sharp!" cried the driver. The signalman tumbled to it at once, asking no further questions.

"Right, mate!" he exclaimed, rushing to the telephone. In three minutes' time the message was transmitted from Sterrington main box to the superintendent's office. In another three minutes they received it at the police station. In five minutes more a sergeant and three constables were pounding along on their bicycles through the silent streets. The open window was a fairly easy thing to find, and as the burglars looked up from their work for the second time that night they stared at the flash of a bull's-eye lantern and felt the snap of handcuffs before they realised what had happened.

"Just in time," said the sergeant, pointing to the safe, the door of which was open.

"Curse you!" muttered one of the men.

"The game's up, Joe," said the other philo-sophically. "There's a young woman in the next room, sergeant; she'll feel a bit more comfortable if you go in and untie her."

They were removing the gag from Maggie's mouth when the sergeant remarked:

"Smart bit o' work. I wonder who gave the alarm."

"*I* did!" exclaimed Maggie triumphantly.

"*You?*"

And then she explained.

*   *   *   *   *   *

When Major and Mrs. Blake returned at a reasonable hour that same morning, they found a policeman on the premises. He announced bluntly that the house had been broken into. The Major began to fume.

"It's that girl and her followers!" he cried, "I knew what would happen."

"Excuse me, sir, but it's owing to your servant and her sweetheart that you haven't lost your stones."

And he told him the story. The Major turned to Maggie, who had come into the hall.

"Well done!" he cried, "I was a bit hasty. Where does that young man live?"

"Please, sir, he's in the kitchen, sir. He came to see how I was."

"Bring him up!" shouted the Major.

Whereupon it fell out that Maggie revoked her month's notice, and that a nice little sum shortly stood to her credit in the Post Office Savings Bank. And as George Ledbury is now fireman of a passenger express, part of that sum will shortly be withdrawn for the purpose of partly furnishing a little house in the railwaymen's quarter of Sterrington.

XIII

WINNING THE RACE

Monsieur de Courcelles, the French Ambassador, sat in the luxurious little study of the French Embassy in London, pale of face, hollow eyed, and with brows knitted in dire perplexity. Those who knew Monsieur de Courcelles in Society, where he was famous for his courteous manners and his subtly humorous *bons môts*, would scarcely have recognised him in the person of this worried and haggard-looking man.

Though, possibly, just the very few men who knew what was going on at some of the embassies at that particular time might have guessed the cause to a certain extent. Diplomatic negotiations of extreme delicacy were being conducted between three of the great European powers, a sort of triangular duel in which each minister for foreign affairs had the interests of his own particular country to think of, together with possible difficulties with the other two.

That morning Monsieur de Courcelles had ventured to smile a little, rub his hands together, and murmur:

"*Bon ! Ca marche bien !*"

Things seemed going smoothly then. And now, at five o'clock in the afternoon, a cypher message had been brought in, which upset all his hopes. He had translated it from the code book himself, and it lay before him, pencilled on a bit of paper, together with a time table. Presently he rang the bell.

A well-dressed young man entered the room. A glance at his chief told him something was wrong. The ambassador shrugged his shoulders, spread out his hands, and exclaimed:

" De Natier left Paris an hour ago. He will be in London to-night—and he carries the Treaty with him."

" But that is good, is it not ? "

" Yes. If I can get that Treaty into the hands of the British Minister before a messenger arrives from Berlin. Otherwise "—he threw out his hands again—" well, you know clause number three will be struck out, though it is to the advantage of both of us."

" Well, there should be no difficulty, *monsieur*. Our information this morning from our Secret Service in Berlin told us there would be a delay, and that no messenger would leave Germany till to-morrow."

The ambassador pushed the paper across the table.

" I have just received this," he said. " Read it."

The Vicomte de St. Croix took the paper and read out loud :

" Von Kriegen left Berlin by Nord Express this morning, crossing Bayende Challover."

He whistled thoughtfully, arching his eyebrows as he did so.

" Which means ? "

" This. De Natier crosses from Belleporte to Fairholt. The boat starts at 7.10 this evening and the train leaves Fairholt at 9.5, arriving in London at 10.45. Von Kriegen takes the Bayende Crossing.

His boat leaves about a quarter to four with a passage of about three and a half hours to Challover. The train leaves Challover at 8.20, arriving in London at 10.20, just twenty-five minutes before De Natier does. The result is obvious."

" You mean that Von Kriegen gets his despatches through the German Ambassador to the Foreign Minister *first* ? "

" Exactly. Which is fatal to us."

The Vicomte de St. Croix, secretary to His Excellency, thought for a moment or two.

" It's the same line, of course," he said, half to himself, " both trains run on the East Southern, only the one from Challover has the start—running through Fairholt twenty-five minutes before De Natier's train starts. As you say," he added, turning to the time table, " it is obvious ! "

" What's to be done ? " asked the ambassador irritably, tapping the table with his pen. " Can *anything* be done to prevent Von Kriegen getting here first, St. Croix ? "

The young man pursed up his lips.

" A motor's out of the question," he said, " so is a special train. De Natier *can't* arrive at Fairholt before the other train has started."

" Can you suggest anything ? "

St. Croix shook his head.

" There's only one thing," he said. " If anyone can help us it's Charlier. He's a wonderful man—especially with his knowledge of railways."

The ambassador looked at his watch.

" Half-past five," he said. " When can you get Charlier here ? "

" I'll telephone to him at once. If he's at home he'll motor down in less than fifteen minutes."

" Yes—telephone immediately. I'd promise him ten thousand francs if he could in any way delay Von Kriegen, without causing complications."

A quarter of an hour later Charlier came and was shown into the private room of St. Croix. He was a short, dark man, with clean shaven face. A Frenchman by nationality on his father's side, Charlier's mother was English, and he himself a mixture. He spoke both languages fluently and without accent, and had long been employed in the French Secret Service as an extremely useful and capable man.

To him St. Croix gave an account of the situation. Charlier took notes carefully. Then he asked to be supplied with an East Southern time table.

" Can you suggest anything ? " asked St. Croix.

Charlier thought for a minute.

" It is a very difficult problem, *monsieur*," he said. " I can't promise anything. If you will allow me, I would like to think it over alone."

" Certainly—but the time ? "

Charlier glanced at the clock on the mantelpiece.

" I know," he said, "there is not a moment to lose. But, unless I have a plan we can do nothing. Stop a minute. Can you send to the East Southern terminus and ask for the conditions of both crossings to-day, and the direction of the wind."

" I'll do so at once," replied St. Croix, leaving the room.

Charlier lit a pipe, spread out a map of the East Southern railway on the table, and then commenced to study it intently, referring every now and then to the time table.

" It's really a little more than twenty-five minutes'

start," he muttered to himself, " the second train is
scheduled a bit faster than the first. I remember
that. Now here's the problem, and a knotty one it
is, too. How to make number two train arrive
before number one. *Can* it be done? Let's see."

Again he squared himself, and pored over the map.

" Could number one train be got out of the way
and number two pass it? Sounds impossible!"

Suddenly his eyes brightened and his finger went
down on a particular place in the map.

"It *is* possible—if the time is short enough.
Twenty-five minutes' interval is too long. Yes—but
how? The job is, how to tackle the interlocking
apparatus."

At this moment St. Croix entered with a
message :

" Strong south-westerly wind, channel passages
up to time, crossing from Bayende to Challover
probably average."

" Good!" exclaimed Charlier, " Von Kriegen's
got the wind against him. If he's only ten minutes
late, that's something. Don't speak—and don't go,
monsieur. I have an idea."

St. Croix watched him. He was making rapid
drawings on a bit of foolscap paper. They looked
liked a jumble of lines and curves. Sometimes he
scribbled a few words against a point in his
drawings.

" Lucky I know the place," he said beneath his
breath.

Suddenly he sat up.

" It *can* be done, *monsieur*," he said.

" What?"

" It is possible that De Natier should arrive
before Von Kriegen, but it's a big risk."

" We—we should not countenance an accident,"
began St. Croix.

" *Monsieur*," interrupted the other, " my plan
entails no accident—not a soul would be hurt in
any way. The risk would be to the men who
undertook the job, and there must be three of us.
If we were discovered, it would mean heavy
imprisonment."

" We would give you ten thousand francs. Can
you find the other men ? "

" Only one—Duquesne. And I must give him at
least a thousand."

" You shall have it, Charlier. And I will offer
my own services."

" I've told you the risk, *monsieur*."

" I'll take it. What is your plan."

Charlier looked at his watch. It was a quarter
to seven.

" There's no time to explain. You have a powerful motor ? "

" A sixty-horse Daimhard."

" Good. Duquesne can drive it. You know
where I live—my flat is close to Westminster
Bridge. Can you be there in half-an-hour ? "

" Yes—I'll drive myself."

" Before you start, send someone to the East
Southern people. Ask them to have a special at
Fairholt on arrival of the boat. You can wire
down to De Natier to take it ? "

" Yes—but even then he'll start *after* Von
Kriegen."

" I know. But he'll get off ten minutes before
the ordinary boat train, and that ten minutes is
everything. Of course, you'll have him met here ? "

" The ambassador will do that."

" Certainly. It's not my affair. I'm going to get him here if I can. In half-an-hour then, *monsieur*. That will give us ample time."

    *   *   *   *   *   *

An hour and a half later a powerful motor was running at high speed along the main road from London to Fairholt, out in the open country. Duquesne was driving, and St. Croix and Charlier occupied the rear seat, the latter explaining the details of as wild a scheme as ever entered his subtle brain.

" I cannot quite understand what you mean by the word interlocking," said St. Croix.

"Apart from technicalities it's really a very simple thing," replied the other. " The idea is this : You want to prevent a signalman from pulling a wrong lever accidentally, and you arrange a series of intricate locks beneath his box so that he is under the control of his own signal apparatus. Let us say that A is the lever which sets the point to run a train off the main line to a branch, and B is the lever which pulls off the semaphore signal. Well, you can't pull B before you've pulled A. The pulling of A unlocks the bar which keeps B rigid."

"Oh, I see."

" So what we're going to do—oh, here we are. I'll soon show you."

They had arrived at a very lonely part of the country where the road ran through a common. A red light here and there betokened the vicinity of a railway, while some four or five hundred yards across the common was a little blaze of light from a signal box.

Charlier spoke to the driver and the car stopped. All lights were extinguished, and they proceeded to

run the car a hundred yards or so over the common.
"No one will suspect it's here," said Charlier.

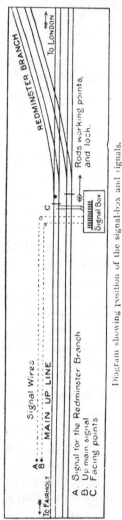

Diagram showing position of the signal-box and signals.

REDMINSTER BRANCH

To LONDON

Rods working points, and lock.

Signal Box

C

a
b

Signal Wires

A ----------
B ----------
MAIN UP LINE

A. Signal for the Redminster Branch
B. Up main signal
C. Facing points

To FAIRHOLT

"Yes, turn her round. We
shall have to run off in a hurry
by and by.   Here are pistols.
They're not loaded, by the way
—only for show. And masks
—we'll put 'em on. Right!
Bring the tools and the wire,
Duquesne."

Then they crept quietly along
towards the signal cabin, passing behind it, and crossing the
line at a point about fifty yards
beyond where two tall signal
posts showed dimly side by
side against the sky, their two
small white back lights shining
in the direction whence the
men had come, and their red
lights glaring towards the down
track.

At the suggestion of Charlier
the three men lay down in
some long grass beside the
track.

"There's plenty of time,"
whispered Charlier, "and I'll
explain the situation. There's
only one man in that box, and
he is stationed there to control the Redminster branch
line which leaves the main

track opposite his cabin.   It's unnecessary to
enter into the complicated details of signalling, but

I must just say that he can't pull the levers to signal a train on to the branch line, until he has first pulled the lever that sets the points which transfer the train off the main line to the branch.

"Now these are the 'home signals,' close by us. Two of them. The inner one is for the main up track and the outer for the branch line. So, when the inner one shows a green light the driver knows the main up line is clear, and when the outer one shows "green" he knows that his train will go on to the Redminster branch. We've only to wait till the up express from Frimwell has gone by. The next train will be the Challover up boat express."

Presently, on the still night air, they heard the bell in the signal box ring.

"The up train," whispered Charlier.

The wire close beside them creaked as it stretched, and the semaphore on the inner post went down with a crash, the red light changing to green. Another wire followed—the back light of the "distant" signal ceased to shine like a star in the darkness.

"Directly she's run by we must set to work," said Charlier. "Duquesne, get the tools ready."

The headlights of the train showed up. Then she passed them with a roar. The signal arm flew up to danger.

"Quick," said Charlier. "Be ready to lend a hand, as I tell you."

Then Charlier did a very curious thing. With his cutters he severed the wires leading from the signal-box to the two signals close by. He took the broken end of the one attached to the main up signal and told Duquesne to make a loop at the end of it. Then he did the same with the end of the *other* wire leading from the cabin. With a bit of the wire he had brought he joined these loops together, the two other men keeping them at a tension. Then he gave Duquesne his final instructions.

" Directly the train has passed, run along the line about a couple of hundred yards on the Red-minster branch. Light the red lamp we've brought and stand it in the six-foot way pointing in the Redminster direction.

" Then hurry back here, and when you see a green light waved from the signal-box, raise this weighted lever at the foot of the up main signal. That will depress the arm. Keep it raised till the next up train runs by, and then rush for the motor, light the lamps, and start the engine. Now, Monsieur de St. Croix! Got your pistol? We'll give our friend the signalman a fright."

    *   *   *   *   *   *

Bill Watson, an oldish man, was making an entry in his log book, when suddenly he heard the door of the cabin open behind him. Turning, his astonished gaze fell upon two masked men, holding revolvers pointed straight at him.

" Don't move! " cried the shorter of the two men, " we won't hurt you, but you've got to do what we tell you."

" What do you want? " asked Watson, with a quick side glance at his telegraph instruments.

" What we *don't* want is for you to give an alarm. Understand, we won't have any nonsense."

" What's your game? Train wrecking or robbery? "

" Neither. We shan't do any damage to anybody or anything. In the first place, remember that I know all the code signals of the East Southern. Keep him covered," he added, turning to St. Croix.

Charlier stepped forward to the row of signal levers, and studied the plan of the junction exposed on a board in front.

In order to make quite sure, he asked a few sharp questions of the signalman, who answered him surlily.

" All right," he exclaimed presently, " now I know just what to do. Hullo! What train's that ? "

" The Challover boat express."

" Good. Accept it—no tricks now ! "

Almost trembling with fear the man gave the "line clear" signal to the previous block, and was about to pull the levers when Charlier pushed him aside.

" I'm going to send that train *on to the branch*."

" You can't," said the man doggedly.

" Can't I ? "

He pulled over two levers. The points opposite changed as they moved. Then he pulled a lever marked "number 6." The signalman grinned a little.

" I don't know what you're up to, but you'll only stop her," he said. "The driver will see you've taken off the branch signal, and he won't run on."

Charlier laughed.

" Look at the back lights," he said.

The man looked and exclaimed :

" Well, I'm blowed ! You've taken off the up main with the branch lever."

" Exactly! Merely a matter of cutting and joining the wires. You must see to that afterwards. Now, what train runs after this ? "

" A special—had a wire about her only half an hour ago," admitted the signalman.

"That's all right. All I want is to get that special in first. Ah, here comes the boat train!"

The head lights—green over white—drew near. She was travelling at sixty miles an hour. On she came. All right! The line was clear. And then, just as she reached the box, she swerved off and went dashing down the branch.

"Signal back 'line clear'!" thundered Charlier, reversing the three levers and pulling over number 1. "She'll go a mile before she pulls up. Good!"

For he saw Duquesne dash past. Three minutes later a warning red light shone on the branch track towards the train that had passed. The driver might back her now, but he would never dare to pass that light witnout explanation. St. Croix, his revolver always pointed at the signalman, waited in tense expectation.

The minutes passed slowly. A series of sharp whistles sounded down the branch. The driver had discovered the mistake.

Five—seven—ten minutes. Then the tail light of the express appeared. She was backing. Another whistle. The red light was seen. Charlier snatched up the cabin lamp, turned on the red shade, and waved it from the door.

"I hope the guard won't run back!" he muttered.

Twelve—fifteen minutes—and then a ring on the bell.

"The special?" exclaimed St. Croix.

"Yes!" cried Charlier. "Take her, man—and send on the line clear—hurry up!"

"You can't get her by," said the man. "You can't pull off the home signal."

Charlier, without a word, turned on the green shade and held out the lamp. The next instant the back light on the up main disappeared. Duquesne had carefully obeyed instructions, and, standing at the foot of the post, had set the signal for the approaching train. Again the bewildered signalman exclaimed; " Well, I'm blowed ! "

" Here she comes ! "

Yes—the violet and green headlights of a special, pacing furiously. The men in charge of the express would understand now why there was a delay in backing on to the main line. At length she reached the signal post and came dashing past the box.

"Off with you ! " cried Charlier to St. Croix. " Sharp. Good-night, my man—you're all right. There's no harm done ! "

The signalman rushed to the door after them as they ran down the steps.

" Help ! " he yelled at the top of his voice. The guard of the express, who had run back, came stumbling over the metals, almost touching St. Croix as the latter vaulted the boundary fence.

" Whiz ! "

Duquesne had reached the motor, started the engine, and was in his seat, steering-wheel in hand. The two men jumped in ; off went the car—bumping over the grass on the common.

" Which way ? " asked Duquesne, as they reached the road.

" London, of course," said Charlier. " Oh, I see what you mean. Better make a bit of a *détour*. We've done our work, and there's no hurry."

＊　　＊　　＊　　＊　　＊　　＊

At the terminus of the East Southern Railway Monsieur de Courcelles himself waited on the platform. Somewhere about ten o'clock he ventured to ask an inspector if the Challover boat express would soon be in.

"No, sir," replied the inspector. "The train's delayed. Something queer seems to have happened down the line, but we don't exactly know what."

"How long will it be?"

"I can't tell you, sir. There's a special from Fairholt due almost directly. Seems to have over-taken the express and passed it somehow."

Then the ambassador knew the situation was saved. In ten minutes' time he was whirling along

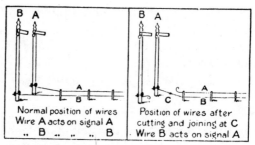

Diagram showing how the wires were cut and rejoined.

towards the Foreign Office, the precious document in his breast pocket.

And, when he left, the document duly signed, he found the German Ambassador's motor had just dashed up.

"You are paying a *late* visit, Baron!" he ex-claimed, as he raised his hat courteously. To which the other replied, under his breath, with a throaty German swear word of several syllables.

A week later the French Ambassador met the British Foreign Minister at a society crush.

"Oh, by the way," said the latter, "a strange thing seems to have happened on one of our railways the night I saw you last. They were talking about it at the Home Office. I gave them a hint, Monsieur de Courcelles, that perhaps it might be as well if Scotland Yard did not press their investigations."

" That was thoughtful of you, my Lord," replied the ambassador, the vestige of a twinkle in his eye.

[Note (for the benefit of railway experts :—

In order to simplify the story I have made no reference to the "distant signals." They would, however, have been worked as follows : For the boat express the "up distant" could not have been taken off, but, of course, the driver would have run by it. For the special, Duquesne would have taken it off, first pulling the lever actuating the "home main," but, in this case, only pulling a broken wire. The interlocking details will readily occur to the expert.]

XIV

THE STRIKERS

THREE third-class coaches were being slowly shunted into the "bay" at the busy station of Maplehurst. There was nothing out of the ordinary in the appearance of these particular coaches, beyond the fact that some of their quarter-lights bore the label, in red lettering, "Reserved," to which was added in a hasty scrawl, " 3.10 p.m. down."

A man, lounging on the platform, eyed them with interest, and then casually inquired of a porter who was going to travel in them, speaking with a slight North country accent.

"Soldiers, I think," was the reply. There was fresh trouble at Northbury last night, and they're going down to stop the row—at least, that's what I've heard."

The other man thanked him quietly for the information, and glanced at his watch. It was about one o'clock. Then he strolled towards a time-table, which he consulted carefully, and with apparent interest in the 3.10 p.m. down train.

He satisfied himself that this train, an express, arrived at Northbury at 4.32, and then he made his way out of the station to the post-office, from which he dispatched a telegram addressed to Northbury.

A smile of satisfaction appeared on his rather sickly and saturnine face as he emerged into the street.

"Well," he said to himself, "at any rate, I've given them due warning of what's going to happen, and I hope they'll take advantage of it. Sending hired butchers—that's what I call it."

That morning the newspapers were full of the strike riots at Northbury. A dispute had occurred, a few weeks previously, between some iron-foundry owners and the workers, and all attempts at settlement had proved futile. Then the trouble had broken out, and mobs of nondescript hooligans had allied themselves to the more discontented of the strikers, and violent measures had been the result. Property was wrecked indiscriminately, machinery damaged, and many of the local police seriously injured.

The authorities—actuated perhaps by humane but, as the sequel had proved, not too wise motives—had been reluctant to call in the aid of the military, and the reinforcements of police from the surrounding district had proved quite inadequate to cope with the tumult. Men's passions had been aroused to a very dangerous degree, and the whole neighbourhood was seething.

What had roused the anger of the strikers especially was the fact that one or two foundries were being partially worked by "blacklegs," and that a few mineral trains laden with pig iron were leaving Northbury daily.

There was already much violent talk of reprisals against the railway company, and the station and sidings at Northbury were carefully guarded by police.

In travelling down to Northbury, one came upon the iron district quite suddenly. A little over an hour's run by express train from Maplehurst was the sleepy old country town of Raebon, situated in the midst of a quiet agricultural district, and showing little sign of life.

Beyond Raebon the railway ran through a lonesome, desolate bit of country, with tracts of heath and woodland and a few scattered houses. There was no station until one reached Tarlington, some eight miles distant from Raebon, and this was only a little wayside place with scant accommodation for any shunting purposes.

Then the train, after running another mile or so, entered a deep cutting through a range of hills, and passed beyond into an entirely different country. Fields and trees and moors seemed to have vanished as if by magic, their places being taken by rows of sidings, the tall chimneys of the foundries, and colonies of little houses, between all of which the train ran till it reached the large and important station of Northbury, three and a half miles beyond Tarlington.

At this same station of Tarlington no one could have guessed, on that particular afternoon, that just over those low hills to the north, half the men of the countryside had gone mad. There was an air of serene repose about the little wayside station. Harding, the station-master and booking-clerk combined, was seated in his office making out returns; Jameson, the solitary porter, was whistling merrily as he trimmed lamps in the porter's room.

At the up end of the platform stood the signal-box, and the stern warning on the outside to the effect that no unauthorised person was allowed therein was being disregarded in the most bare-faced manner in the person of Johnny Harding, the station-master's small boy, aged ten, who was enjoying his Saturday holiday in the company of Crake, the signalman, and more especially those moments of it when Crake allowed him to return a call or to pull over such of the levers as yielded to his boyish strength.

Truth to tell, Johnny knew as much about the working of the Tarlington box as Crake did himself. The boy was a railway enthusiast, and could tell you the name or number of every engine on the system, and had the code signals by heart, to say nothing of the scheduled time of every train, stopping and express, that ran through the station, with an accuracy of memory equal to the "working time-table" itself.

The bell suddenly rang out, the "be-ready" signal. Crake returned it. Then he went to the telephone.

"What is it?" asked the boy.

"An up mineral train just leaving Northbury," replied the signalman as he hung up the receiver.

"Minerals" were running anyhow that week. Crake accepted it, and a little disc marked "train on line" appeared in the instrument in front of him. The "mineral" had started from Northbury.

The boy took up the pen on the booking-desk, and glanced at the clock. All movements of trains have to be entered carefully.

"3.36," he said, as he wrote it down; "how about the 3.58 slow passenger train from North-bury?"

"She's to pass the mineral train here," replied Crake.

Which meant that the mineral train was to be

shunted off the up main line at Tarlington to allow of the passage of the slow passenger train, and was then to follow the latter.

The boy took a glance out of the window. There was a "refuge siding," leading back from the up main line, and this siding was full of empty trucks. The accommodation at Northbury was becoming limited, and these trucks were an "overflow."

"There won't be room," he said presently.

"Doesn't matter," replied Crake, as he pulled off the home signal, "the down main's clear for the next-half hour or more. She can go into that for the time being."

Heavy wreaths of steam came puffing up through the cutting. The mineral train came lumbering along. The driver shut off steam and crawled through the station, bringing his engine to a standstill opposite the box.

Crake slid the window open and looked out. The train was a heavy one.

"You'll have to go on the down main," he said.

"Right!" answered the driver, exactly understanding the situation.

"How are things going yonder?" asked the signalman, jerking his thumb in the direction of Northbury.

"Bad, mate—bad as can be. They've lost their heads. We shouldn't ha' got out half an hour later—there ain't enough police to stop 'em. There's a talk o' the soldiers coming down."

"Pretty nigh time something was done," replied Crake, who had little sympathy with the strikers.

"You're right, mate. Well, I'm glad I shall be out of it to-night."

He started the engine and the train moved slowly on, coming to a halt when it had gone a few hundred yards. Then Crake pulled the necessary levers and signalled with his arm through the box. The train came back, crossing over to the down line, and remained stationary alongside the platform. Thus the up line was made clear for the coming passenger train.

In a few minutes the train from Northbury was signalled, the station-master and the porter appeared on the up platform, together with three or four passengers, and the train came in.

It was just at this moment that Johnny, looking out of the signal-box, caught sight of a dense black mass coming along the road down the hill; as the train moved out of the station the sound of singing arose.

"Look there!" exclaimed the boy, "what's up?"

Crake threw back the starting signal lever and glanced out of the box. A crowd of men was rushing down the hill towards the station, singing and shouting.

"Hullo!" he cried, "they must be some of the Northbury lot—what are they doing here?"

Remembering his duty, however, he turned towards his instruments again. It has been said that the next station on the up line was Raebon, but the next "block" was a little signal-box half-way between the two stations known as "Tedworth level-crossing."

There were no sidings or cross-over points at this box; it merely guarded the level-crossing of the country road which gave it its name. Crake waited till the bell warned him that the passenger train had passed this box; he returned this signal,

H

and the disc in the "up" instrument changed from "train on line" to "line clear." He could now

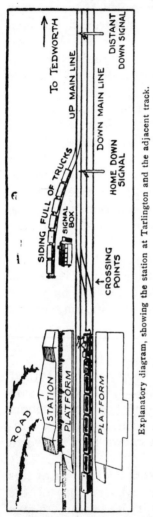

Explanatory diagram, showing the station at Tarlington and the adjacent track.

send the mineral train forward.

He had already pulled over the levers once more for this purpose when the crowd of men and hooligans burst into the station. Before they knew what had happened, the unfortunate station-master and porter found themselves seized by rough hands and forced into the porter's room, and the key was turned upon them.

Crake stood, hand on the lever he had just turned over, thunderstruck. The boy's quicker wits grasped the situation—or, at least, part of it.

"Quick—the telephone!" he cried.

Crake turned to the instrument when half-a-dozen men rushed up the steps and invaded the cabin. Johnny, half from fear, slid behind the desk and crouched down on the floor.

"No you don't!" exclaimed a tall, stalwart man, evidently the leader, as he struck down Crake's hand from the bell push. "We're not going to do you any harm, mate, if you keep quiet and do as you're told—if not, you'll bring it on yourselves. Tie him up, lads!"

In two minutes Crake was bound down to the solitary chair the box contained. The boy breathed hard behind the desk. He was not discovered.

"Now," said the leader, "which of you chaps said you knew how to work these things?" and he pointed to the instruments and levers.

"I did, Sinclair," said a short man, stepping forward, "I was on the line myself once."

"Right. Then see to it that no messages get through—and that the down express comes along— d'ye understand, Macpherson?"

"Aye! I can get her through—if that's what you want, mate."

"It's not quite what I want," exclaimed the other, "I haven't made up my mind yet—the first thing to do is to clear out this pig iron. I'll be back directly."

Outside, the mob had already attacked the hated mineral train. The driver, seeing the points rightly set, had attempted to start, but was quickly dragged off the footplate together with the fireman. Sinclair stood on the little platform outside the box, surveying the scene. They were letting down the sides of the trucks, and the heavy pigs of iron came crashing out upon the platform on one side and the six-foot way on the other.

An ugly expression came over the face of the strike leader. Three days' rioting had turned him from a usually phlegmatic north countryman into a brute, and there was a gleam of murder in his grey eyes. Within his breast pocket was a certain telegram which he had received from Maplehurst a few hours previously.

They were going to send soldiers down, were they? Soldiers who might possibly fire upon him and his comrades. Let them see to it, then. If anything happened they would bring it upon their own heads, curse them!

Suddenly he turned and came back into the signal-box.

" What time does the down express pass Raebon ? " he asked Crake abruptly.

" 4.17," replied the signalman sullenly.

Sinclair looked at the clock. It was very nearly that time now.

" And what time does she run through here ? "

" 4.29."

Sinclair went out again and shouted to the madmen below. They stopped in their work of destruction.

" Let's hear Sinclair ! " cried a voice.

" Ah, hear me, lads ! " shouted the ringleader. " There's a train coming down—it's nearly due now—with three carriages full of soldiers. D'ye know what *that* means ? "

Wild yells of execration answered him.

" Once they're let loose on ye," he went on, " there'll be murder done. But I've a plan for stopping them. Leave yon train in the way, and they'll have to stop here. There are a couple of hundred of us. We can storm the carriages before they know where they are and break up their rifles. Who's game ? "

Wild voices answered him and hoarse cheers rose from the maddened crowd.

" We'll do it, mate ! "

" Right. *What are you doing with the engine ?* "

He had suddenly seen some of the men uncoupling the engine of the mineral train, while one had sprung on the footplate. It was just at this precise moment that the bell rang out in the cabin and Macpherson received the signal from Tedworth level-crossing box that the express had left Raebon.

In obedience to the orders of Sinclair he began to pull the levers which actuated the signals for the express. But they would not move because they had been locked by Crake when the latter pulled the two levers to shunt the mineral train from the down to the up line. Macpherson saw this and replaced these two levers. He could now set the signals for the express.

" Good heavens, man," exclaimed Crake, observing what was going on—" there's a train standing there—on the down road."

" I know there is," said Macpherson, pulling off the home and distant signals. " That's our game. When the driver sees it he'll stop the express—don't you worry, mate."

" What are you doing with the engine ? " cried Sinclair once more.

" Going to send her up the line," answered the man on the footplate, " she shan't have a chance of drawing a mineral train this journey."

" Stop, you fool ! " thundered Sinclair.

But the man had already opened the throttle valve and jumped off the footplate. The great engine began to move forward.

" Good heavens ! " screamed Macpherson, seeing what was happening, " the crossing points are not set ! She'll run into the express ! "

The old habit had come back to him. He was

no longer the mad ironworker on strike, but the signalman on duty.

But it was too late now for him to transfer the engine to the other line. The heavy locomotive gathering speed, took the down metals, and rushed forward to meet the express *on the same line of rails.* Sinclair saw what had happened in a moment. He also grasped the fact of the awful catastrophe that must take place when the two engines met. And a thrill of diabolical joy welled through him. Let it happen, then! No human power could prevent it now.

"Clear out, Macpherson!" he cried. Then, addressing the mob, who stood paralysed on trucks and platforms, he shouted:

"Out of the station, lads! Back home, every one of you!"

There was a scramble out of the trucks and across metals and platforms. A panic seemed to have seized the men as they realised the horrible thing that was going to happen. They poured out of the station faster than they had entered it, leaving Harding the station-master, the porter, driver, and fireman under lock and key, and the signalman fast bound.

The only other railway official, the brakesman of the mineral train, had long since jumped from his van and hurried back along the line towards North-bury to summon assistance.

One person, and one person only was left free at the station, and that was Johnny Harding. He came out from behind the desk, ghastly pale, but with all his wits about him. And he flew to the telephone.

"It's too late," said Crake, "nothing can save the express now. Look at the clock!"

The clock marked 4.20. The express was approaching from Raebon at full speed—and the engine of the goods train, a tiny speck in the distance now, was rushing forward to meet it.

Nevertheless, in sheer desperation, the boy pushed the little knob to ring up Tedworth level-crossing box—where the express was due at 4.22.

* * * * * *

Old Joe Salter sat in his little box at Tedworth level-crossing, stirring the fire in his stove with his wooden leg. Years before, he had lost a leg in the company's service, and was relegated to his present post, which was a light one. He had to open and shut the gates of his crossing, and act as the mid-way "block" between Raebon and Tarlington. His signal cabin, with its five levers, two each for up and down home and distant signals, and one for locking his gates, was on the ground level.

He had received the signal that the express had left Raebon, and duly accepted it and passed it on to Tarlington. His gates were open to the line, and his down signals pulled off. All was right. Over one of the gates hung a youth, with a team of horses behind him, drawing a felled tree trunk on a low waggon, waiting till the train had passed. It would do so in another two minutes, for it was just 4.20 o'clock, and the train was well up to time.

Suddenly there came a ring at the bell. Somebody wanted to speak to him from Tarlington. He rose, went to the telephone, and gave the answering ring. Then he raised the instrument to his ear. Johnny Harding's voice came through.

"Stop the express—quick—stop the express."

It was unusual, but the old man never stayed to question it. "Clang—clang" back went the two levers, and two signal arms rose to "danger," one, the distant, half-a-mile up the line, and the other about three hundred yards from his box, in the same direction. The express might pass the "distant," but not the "home."

He returned to the telephone.

"What's the matter, then?" he asked.

His face blanched as the appalling news came through.

"The strikers—they've sent on a goods engine—on the down metals—by itself—no one on footplate—it'll wreck the express—can you do anything?"

The old man dropped the receiver, dazed for a moment. Then he shouted back:

"When did it start?"

"Four or five minutes ago—can you do anything?"

Joe Salter gazed round wildly. Then the inspiration came.

"Yes!" he shouted, and threw back the locking lever.

The next moment he was stumping over the lines to the gates. The whistle of the express sounded, shrieking for its right of way. He glanced in the other direction. A puff of white rose above the distant trees. Hauling the gates open, he cried to the astonished youth:

"Bring your lot across—quick! There's no time for question—hurry up, lad!"

Wondering dimly why a train should be stopped to make way for his load, the yokel gee'd up his horses and led them forward slowly. The great tree trunk was across the down metals.

"Stop—unlatch the chain your side—look alive, sonny—I'll see to this one."

The chain traces were quickly loosed.

"Now!" thundered the old man, "off with those horses—for your life, lad! Lash them up!"

Just then the goods engine rounded a curve and came thundering along. The youth, his dull brain roused at last, needed no further warning. He struck out with his whip at the horses, and ran after them as they plunged at a gallop along the road, followed by old Joe Salter stumping along as fast as his wooden leg would allow him.

As the crash came, he turned. It was an appalling sight. The great engine ran full tilt into the waggon and tree trunk, seemed to push both out of its way, literally staggered on, tearing up metals and throwing ballast in clouds, shook, tottered, thundered, and hissed. Finally it rolled over on its side, a mass of metal, steam, and flying wheels, dragging itself many yards along the side of the line, breathing its dying breath in the form of a white cloud of vapour intermixed with glowing embers.

The express was saved—by not much more than a hundred yards!

*　　*　　*　　*　　*　　*

Half-an-hour later the breakdown train, with its wonderful hydraulic crane and lifts, came down from Northbury, and a gang of men set to work instantly to clear the road of the masses of *débris*, and to lay rails for the passage of the express over the ruined gap. Long before then soldiers and passengers had clustered round the plucky old man to whom they owed their lives, and not one of them grudged his coin when the hat went round.

The soldiers reached Northbury several hours

late, but their services were not required that night. A fear—a horror had run through the hearts of the more violent of the strikers. Besides which, they wanted leaders, and Sinclair and Macpherson were nowhere to be found, then or at any other time.

A week later two persons "trod the carpet" in the General Manager's office, an old wooden-legged man and a small boy. And the "G. M.," when he had finished his complimentary speech, which was accompanied by something else of a substantial nature, remarked:

"Well, Salter, I think it's time you were placed in honourable retirement—you've well earned it. As for you, Johnny, I hope you *won't* retire. We must make a railway man of you, my boy, later on. And I hope you'll never have to sacrifice an engine to save an express again. But it was worth it, and the company is proud of the services of both of you!"

XV

THE RUSE THAT SUCCEEDED

A SPICK and span little steam yacht was slowly
entering the tiny harbour of Porthaven. The tide
was ebbing fast and the pier master shouted a few
directions, for the channel of available water was
not very wide. She flew the French tricolour flag
astern, and the pennant of a weil-known French
yacht club on her foremast. On the bridge, smoking
a cigarette, stood a little man, every bit as spick
and span as the yacht herself; a typical Frenchman,
dressed in a spotless white duck suit, with very
sharp, piercing brown eyes which scanned the quay-
side narrowly.

There was nothing remarkable in the entrance of
a French yacht into the little harbour of Porthaven.
It was the height of the yachting season, and a
dozen other small private craft lay there at anchor,
or were moored alongside the quay. The owner of
one of them, standing on deck with a pair of glasses,
remarked to a lady who stood by his side:

" That's *Hirondelle* coming in. She belongs to a
chap named De Natoye—there he is, on the bridge.
I met him at Cannes this spring."

" A Frenchman ? "

" Yes—and a rich one too. A very jolly chap.
I'll have the dinghy out and pay him a call when
he comes to anchor. Welcome him to English
waters."

For the next few days De Natoye was welcomed
not only by this particular owner of a yacht, but
also by everyone of note in Porthaven. He was an
agreeable little man, bright and vivacious, and his
presence added much to the society gathered at the
seaside resort. Once or twice he pleaded excuses
for not accepting invitations to lunch or dinner, and
on these occasions it might have been noticed that
he took an express to London, and was not arrayed
in yachting garb.

But with Monsieur De Natoye himself and his
elegant steam yacht this story does not deal directly,
although he was the leading cause that led to a
curious railway incident. It will be necessary,
therefore, to leave *Hirondelle* at her moorings in
Porthaven harbour, and to transfer the scene
to London—hot and out of season at the end of
August.

Night had set in when, out of one of the little
side streets in that strange district called Soho, there
came into Wardour Street an unobtrusive little man,
who glanced once or twice over his shoulders as if
to see whether anyone were following him or not.
A look of satisfaction passed over his face as he
made up his mind that, apparently, he was unobserved. Porthaven yachtsmen, looking at him
closely, would have noticed that he was Monsieur
De Natoye, and would have remembered that he
had refused, with most polite excuses, to attend a
dinner that night on board Lord Feverel's yacht
Firefly.

Arrived in Piccadilly Circus he lit a cigarette,
unbuttoned the light dust-coat he was wearing,
disclosing an expanse of shirt-front beneath, and
strolled leisurely in the direction of a famous *café*,

where men of all nations congregate. It being out of the season, there were not many present.

Seated in a corner, a Benedictine on the table in front of him, a cigar in his mouth, was a tall, military-looking man, with a big moustache and keen grey eyes. Anyone who knew anything of the diplomatic world would have recognised him at once as Colonel Sibthorpe, attached to the Foreign Office, " a deuced good berth, and nothing to do, what ? " as some of his military friends said.

In fact, no one seemed to know quite what the Colonel's exact mission was. He made pleasant little Continental tours, he lounged about town, was an agreeable companion, and knew what was going on in the world. That was all most men could say about him.

Monsieur de Natoye walked up to him. The Colonel nodded affably.

" Hullo ! " he exclaimed, " *you* in town ? What brings you to this dull metropolis ? "

" Business—a leetle business, Colonel," answered the Frenchman, sitting down beside him.

The Colonel motioned to a waiter.

" A Benedictine ? " he asked.

" Certainly. Thank you."

" Bring me another, too."

" Yessir."

When the drinks arrived the Colonel, leaning back in the chair, said nonchalantly in a low tone :

" Well ? Settled it ? "

" Yes," answered De Natoye, sinking his voice to the level of the other.

" When ? "

" Wednesday."

" What time ? "

" He takes the 7.15 train from London."

" And reaches Porthaven ? "

" At 10.42."

" You sail at once ? "

" No.   The tide will not serve before half-past one in the morning."

The Colonel puffed at his cigar thoughtfully.

" Anyone suspect ? " he asked presently.

" We think not, but we are not sure."

" Humph."

" You will help us ? "

" Only as far as I can—you know my position ? "

The Frenchman nodded.   Someone sat down at the next table, a foreigner apparently.   The Colonel raised his voice.

" You are staying in town to-night ? "

" Yes."

" Ah !   Glad to have seen you.   I must be off. Good-night ! "

He finished his liqueur, shook hands with De Natoye, strolled outside on the pavement, and hailed a taxi.

" Kensington High Street."

" Whereabouts, sir ? "

" Oh, the station will do."

Arrived there, he got out, dismissed the taxi, and walked some little distance in the Hammersmith direction till he came to a row of ugly-looking houses standing back from the street.   Taking a quick glance on either side first, he went up to the door of one of these houses and rang the bell.   The servant came.

" Mr. Brett at home ? "

" Yes, sir, but I think he's engaged."

The Colonel took a card from his pocket, a blank

one, wrote a few words upon it, and handed it to her.

" Give him that and I think he'll see me."

In less than a minute the servant was showing him into a room at the back of the house. An alert-looking, clean-shaven man of middle height rose from the desk at which he was seated.

" I didn't expect you, sir," he said quietly.

"No," replied the Colonel as he took a seat, " but I've a bit of work on hand that I think requires your services."

Brett closed the door and locked it, his face betraying no surprise. He was accustomed to secret commissions from the Foreign Office; in fact he made his living chiefly by this means. Not that he stood in any official capacity. He knew very well the risks he ran, and that if he walked into trouble he could expect no open help from those whom he served. The secret agent of a Government often has important work to do, and does it well as a trusted servant, but he must never expect to be recognised officially.

The Colonel lit a cigar, took a notebook from his pocket, and consulted it carefully. Presently he said :

" You know a man named Koravitch—a Russian, don't you ? "

Brett thought for a moment. Then he replied :

" Yes. Goes by the name of Martin sometimes."

The Colonel nodded. Brett unlocked a cabinet and took a small, indexed book from it.

" Here he is," he said presently, " Koravitch, Russian subject. A suspect in Russia. Gave information on Roumanian question. Known to the French Secret Service. Useful man."

The Colonel nodded.

" That's the chap," he said, " do you happen to know where he is now ? "

Brett again consulted his notebook.

" Yes—in England—unless he's left the country during the last fortnight—which would have been difficult," he added grimly.

" It would have been difficult, as you say," replied the Colonel.   " I see you're up-to-date, Brett."

" It's my business, sir. Do you want Koravitch ? I can soon lay my hand on him."

" So can I.   But we don't want him just now. Let me give you the facts of the case.   Koravitch, as you said just now, is a useful man—both to us and the French Government.   But the Russians don't want him on the Continent.   They know very well he's here—they made it too hot for him in his own country—and the Russian police have been keeping him under observation.   But as long as he remains in England they'll leave him alone.   Well, as it happens, there's a very good reason why he should go to France just now."

" I see—and you want me to get him over there quietly ? "

" No, I don't.   That's the affair of the French Secret Service, not ours.   And it's been arranged. You know Monsieur De Natoye ? "

Brett's eyes sparkled.

" One of the cleverest little fellows they've got."

" Quite so.   Well, he's got a yacht lying at Porthaven, ready to take Koravitch off.   I owe him a good turn, and although, as I said, the affair is not ours, and we can't take any definite action, still I'm anxious he shculd get Koravitch away."

" What do you want me to do, sir ? "

"The case stands thus. Directly the Russian police suspect the man's leaving England, they'll arrest him. They've got a plausible reason—so plausible that international complications would arise if any department went to the Home Office and stopped interference."

"You mean, sir, that our police would have to help the Russians if called upon ?"

"Exactly. They're hardly likely to do that—I don't think they will—but our police must be kept out of it. Now, Koravitch takes the 7.15 train to Porthaven at the terminus of the London Eastern and Porthaven line on Wednesday night. He arrives there at 10.42, but De Natoye's yacht can't get out before one, because of the tide. What the Russian police will do, if they suspect anything, is this. They'll either have Koravitch arrested before he leaves London, or they'll go down to Porthaven and nab him on the boat. He's not out of the wood till the yacht starts. Then De Natoye will see to it."

" What do you want me to do, sir ? "

"If you can, shadow the whole thing unostentatiously, and, if there is a danger of the arrest taking place, prevent it. You'll earn a big fee. But, remember, I can give you no support in any way."

"That's understood, sir. Anyhow I'll try my best."

The Colonel shrugged his shoulders.

" Right ! You know your game then. Don't come to me about it—at all events, until Thursday, when it will have been played out one way or another. Good night ! "

*   *   *   *   *   *

Turning over the papers on the bookstall at the

London terminus of the London Eastern and Port-haven Railway stood Brett, apparently a nondescript individual with plenty of time on his hands. But he was by no means idle. The centre of observation was the gateway to number 7 platform close by, from which the 7.15 express to Porthaven started. It was just after seven now, and the train was drawn up in readiness. Brett scrutinised quietly every person who went through the gate. He also kept his eyes from time to time on the door leading from the booking office, and took searching glances round the big open space between the station buildings and the entrances to the various platforms.

At ten minutes past seven a man walked quickly across this space to where Brett was standing ; it was one of his subordinates.

" All right," he said, " he's taking his ticket. I followed him all the way in a taxi."

" See anyone ? "

" No."

" They're artful," replied Brett, " I've had to deal with them before. Go outside and watch everyone who comes to the station. If you see them, come at once. If we can, we must stop them somehow."

The man went back. In a couple of minutes an individual came across to platform number 7, a man with a large head and wearing a soft hat turned down over his forehead. Brett recognised him by his walk.

" Koravitch ! " he said to himself. " I expect the poor beggar feels precious nervous."

He watched him take a seat in the train. A sudden thought occurred to him. He glanced at the clock. It was now 7.10.

" Allow me to speak to a friend who is leaving by this train ? "

" Certainly, sir," said the polite official, letting him through the gate.

He went up to the carriage. The man within gave a start as Brett's head poked itself into the window.

" All right," said the latter, " I know. The coast is clear, but if they should come at the last moment drop out on the other side and let them board the train. If not, when you get down make your friend take his yacht out the instant the tide serves. That's all."

Without waiting for a reply he hurried back to his post of observation and watched the clock.

Twelve minutes past—thirteen—fourteen—surely it was all right now.

No! Suddenly he saw his fellow detective rushing across. He ran forward to meet him.

" Three of them! " said the man.

" Right. Charge! " exclaimed Brett, in a low voice.

Three men came dashing out of the booking office close on each other's heels. Without a word Brett and his assistant rushed forward with their heads down to meet them. As they did so Brett heard the bell ring at the platform entrance.

They tilted against the first man, fell in a heap, and the other two came tripping over them. There was a little chorus of strange oaths ; one of the men picked himself up and made a dash for number 7 platform.

" Too late, sir," said the collector, indicating, with a jerk of his thumb, the outgoing train.

" I don't know whether you ought to apologise

to us, or we to you," said Brett, blandly, " the meeting was so mutual ! "

The leader of the three men looked at him with a scowl of suspicion. Brett raised his hat politely, and passed on, remarking :

"*I* don't mind apologising. I'm very sorry to have caused you any inconvenience."

" That's all right," said his subordinate, as they passed out of the station.

" Not a bit of it," replied Brett.

" What do you mean ? "

" If they've as much common sense as I have— and I certainly give them credit for that—they'll find an easy way out of the difficulty."

" But it's the last train to Porthaven ! "

" On *this* line," said Brett, drily. " Come in here and have a drink. This thing's got to be thought out."

Brett explained as they sat in the corner of a private bar.

" The case is like this," he said. " There's one way, and only one way of getting to Porthaven to-night before the yacht sails, and it's this. You know Melfield, don't you ? "

" Yes. About a hundred miles down the line, isn't it ? "

" That's right. A local train leaves Melfield at 11.5, arriving at Porthaven just after half-past twelve. If they catch *that*, Koravitch won't get out of the country."

" But how *can* they catch it ? "

" By taking the 9.5 on the South Midland Railway to Melfield. It arrives there at 10.48. The South Midland and the London Eastern and Porthaven stations at Melfield are just over a mile apart. They'd do it easily if they took a motor."

" I see—but not if the train were late ? "

" That train never is late. It nearly always runs to time."

" If it could be delayed on the journey—— "

" Exactly," replied Brett. " That's just the problem I'm trying to work out. I want to delay that train and I want to do it without any risk of danger to anyone—that is, of course, if they travel by it—as I think they will. And there isn't much time."

He lit his pipe and smoked thoughtfully for a few minutes. Then a smile came into his face.

" I know something about railways," he said, "and the way they're worked. And I have an idea I can make that train late at Melfield."

" How ? "

" With a good strong gimlet ! "

" A *gimlet* ? "

" I haven't time to explain. You go straight to the South Midland Terminus and keep a look-out. Don't let them see you. At ten minutes to nine you'll see me by the bookstall—I shall be dressed as an old man. Let me know if they are there. That's all. I've just got time to run home and change first."

Before he called a taxi to take him home, Brett entered a shop close by and purchased a large, strong gimlet, with a sharp screw point, carefully examining it to see that it was good steel.

About a quarter to nine an old man walked slowly into the terminus of the South Midland Railway. Clouds had come over the evening sky, and darkness had set in prematurely. He loitered about by the bookstall till his subordinate came up.

" You were right," said the latter, " they're all three here, and they've taken tickets for Melfield."

"Good! You needn't wait. If you like to come to my house in an hour's time I'll explain things to you."

The South Midland Terminus is constructed on a different principle from that of the London Eastern and Porthaven, in that passengers have free access to all the platforms. Brett made his way to number 4, from which he ascertained the Melfield train started. It was just being slowly backed in, the red tail light gleaming as it came down the line to the buffer stops at the "dead end." Brett knew that the chief difficulty of his task was to escape the notice of the officials. He entered a compartment at the rear end of the train, crossed the floor of the carriage, opened the further door, and, closing it behind him, dropped down on the line beyond, between the train and another that stood on the neighbouring metals.

Then he made his way cautiously to the back of the train and crawled under the last coach, coming out behind it—between it and the "dead end." It was fairly dark here, with the exception of the gleam from the red lamp.

It was this red lamp that Brett wanted—for less than a minute. Making up his mind for a bold attempt he reached for it, removed it from its socket behind the coach, put it on the ground, and, stooping down, removed the lamp itself from its outer case. Then, with a sharp prod from his gimlet, he bored a hole at the bottom of the oil receptacle, giving the tool a quick turn afterwards. The oil came dripping out.

In ten seconds the leaking lamp was replaced on its socket, and Brett was under the coach again. He managed to slip out unobserved, and to gain platform number 5 through the other train. Before he left the station he saw the three Russian police agents enter the Melfield express. Then he went home satisfied, saying to himself:

" Even if they order a special to Porthaven at Melfield they can't get there in time. It would take too long to get one out. I should like to be on that train and see the effect."

The effect was very simple. A red tail light is placed at the rear of a train for several reasons—to protect it should it be at a standstill, and, more especially, to notify to signalmen on duty that the whole of the train has passed, and that the line behind, therefore, is clear.

Slowly, but surely, the oil trickled out of that particular lamp, until none was left. The train had run some fifty or sixty miles of its journey when the light finally drooped and went out. The first man who noticed something was wrong was the signalman in charge of an obscure roadside cabin named " Cherrington Box." He gave a little start as the train whisked by, and then promptly obeyed his printed orders. That is to say, he went to his signalling apparatus, and sent forward to the next box the code signal of his line, seven beats, a pause, and a final beat. In the next signal-box the man on duty heard the eight rings in this particular order, and, to his ears, they carried the very plain message:

" Stop and examine train ! "

Which he proceeded to do by keeping the home signal against her.

" What's up ? " cried the driver, as he stopped beside the box.

" Cherrington telephones you've got no tail ' light," shouted the signalman.

Down jumped the guard and ran behind the train. The lamp was there right enough, but out. He tried to light it, and swore at the lampmen fifty miles behind him.

"Forgot to fill it!" he muttered.

In his van was a spare one. But it took several minutes before it was fixed behind the train. Three men were anxious, and one of them shouted out of the window to the front guard, with a foreign accent:

"Why do we stop?"

"All right, sir; we're just off."

"We shall be late at Melfield?"

"Yes, sir, I'm afraid we shall."

"A sovereign if we're in time."

"Hope we shall be, then," said the guard; "but it doesn't rest with me. Right away, George! Try your best, and it's shares."

For he guessed the driver had overheard. But, at Slade Junction box, a cross-country express, well up to time, got the road on to Melfield first, and the London train steamed in thirteen minutes late. For the second time that night three men failed to get to Porthaven, and perhaps they guessed it was not pure accident.

On Friday Brett saw Colonel Sibthorpe.

"Well," said the latter, "he got off all right. I suppose the coast was clear after all?"

"I rather fancy *I* made it clear for him," replied Brett, with a smile.

"How?"

He drew a gimlet from his pocket and showed it to the Colonel.

"With this, sir."

And he proceeded to explain.

What my Mirror Showed me — Before I used Antipon.

THE MODERN METHOD OF CURING OBESITY.

What my Mirror Showed me — When I had used Antipon.

THE days when obesity was generally regarded as an incurable disease are long gone by; we could also wish that the erroneous idea that obesity can be cured by starving and exercising were consigned to limbo; but popular fallacies die hard. Obesity can no more be cured by depriving the body of a sufficiency of nourishment, or by unduly fatiguing it by physical exertion, than anæmia can be cured by such means. Nor are mineral or other drug remedies the least good. The fact is, obesity implies a weak condition of body, however stout and rubicund a person may be; and to cure it *we must go to the root of the evil, take Antipon, feed up well,* and so effect a sort of transformation.

Antipon, famous as a fat-reducer, is also a fine tonic, revivifying the entire system, and having a special stimulating and strengthening effect on the digestive machinery. It creates an excellent appetite, and, the wholesome food taken being thoroughly assimilated, the whole organism is renourished and reinvigorated.

"Obesity," says one of our greatest physicians, "is a general state of disordered nutrition of the body, characterised by an excessive development of the adipose tissue, which leads to various disturbances of the bodily functions." Therefore Antipon, by repairing the physical conditions on which nutrition depends, and by rapidly eliminating all the needless fatty deposits, completely cures the disease of obesity, reinvigorates the muscular and nervous systems, and restores health and strength generally. The limbs, waist, hips, etc., become firm, slender, and nicely shaped, while the disfiguring fat about the cheeks, chin, neck, etc., quickly falls away, leaving beauty and delicacy of contour. The complexion and skin are greatly benefited by the action of Antipon through the enriched blood.

Antipon is purely vegetable in composition, but liquid in form.

Antipon is sold in bottles, price 2s. 6d. and 4s. 6d., by Chemists, Stores, etc., or may be had (on sending remittance), privately packed, carriage paid in the United Kingdom, direct from the Antipon Company, Olmar Street, London, S.E.

Antipon can be had from stock or on order from all Druggists and Stores in the Colonies and India, and is stocked by wholesale houses throughout the world.

PEARSON'S
ARE THE BEST

Volumes by all the leading Authors are

Adventures of Captain Kettle	C. J. Cutcliffe Hyne
The Adventures of Nell Gwyn	F. Frankfort Moore
David Harum	E. N. Westcott
Sir George Tressady	Mrs. Humphry Ward
The Skipper's Wooing	W. W. Jacobs
The New Rector	Stanley Weyman
The Chronicles of Don Q.	K. & H. Prichard
The Wrong Box	Robert Louis Stevenson and Lloyd Osbourne
A Desperate Conspiracy	Guy Boothby
Cleopatra	Rider Haggard
Doreen: The Story of a Singer	Edna Lyall
The Angel of the Revolution	George Griffith
Just as I am	M. E. Braddon
Mord Em'ly	W. Pett Ridge
The Invisible Man	H. G. Wells
Meadowsweet and Rue	Silas K. Hocking
Willowdene Will	Halliwell Sutcliffe
The Beetle: A Mystery	Richard Marsh
Convict 99	Marie Connor and Robert Leighton
The Strange Disappearance of Lady Delia	Louis Tracy
Mystery of a Hansom Cab	Fergus Hume
The Face of Clay	Horace Annesley Vachell
Rachel Marr	Morley Roberts

Price **6d.** each, of all Booksellers, or post free (inland) **8d.** each;
C. ARTHUR PEARSON, Ltd.,

SIXPENNY NOVELS
HOLIDAY READING

included. HERE IS A SELECTION :—

The Log of a Sea Waif	FRANK BULLEN
Senator North	GERTRUDE ATHERTON
A Modern Juliet	CHARLES GARVICE
Young April	EGERTON CASTLE
The Raiders	S. R. CROCKETT
Maisie's Romance	E. M. ALBANESI
Graham of Claverhouse	IAN MACLAREN
The Trespasser	GILBERT PARKER.
Cold Steel	M. P. SHIEL
Lovers of Yvonne	RAFAEL SABATINI
The Visits of Elizabeth	ELINOR GLYN
Diamond Cut Paste	A. & E. CASTLE
New Chronicles of Don Q.	K. & H. PRICHARD
The Yarn of Old Harbour Town	W. CLARK RUSSELL
The Triumph of Love	EFFIE ADELAIDE ROWLANDS
A Daughter of the Reds	MAX PEMBERTON
Stranleigh's Millions	ROBERT BARR
The Ending of my day	" RITA "
Devil's Dice	W. LE QUEUX
Bam Wildfire	HELEN MATHERS
St. Veda's	ANNIE S. SWANN
Fetters of Fire	BERTHA M. CLAY
The Phantom of the Opera	GASTON LEROUX

A complete list of upwards of 200 titles will be sent on application.

three volumes for **1s. 10d.**, six for **3s. 4d.**, twelve for **6s. 6d.**, from
17 and 18, Henrietta Street, London, W.C.

CONCERNING TATCHO

WHEN President Lincoln was asked to take the wrong side of a case he said, "I could not do it. All the time while talking to that jury I should be thinking, 'Lincoln, you're a liar, you're a liar,' and I believe I should forget myself and say it out loud."

Truth and honesty made Lincoln the giant he became.

"Truth shall be thy warrant."

Photo by] **Mr. GEO. R. SIMS.** [*Lavis.*

There is no advertisement in the world that can compare with that which comes from the reputation of always and everywhere being absolutely reliable.

When Mr. Geo. R. Sims discovered the hair grower, he christened it under the Romany name of Tatcho.

Why?

Because this word Tatcho literally means what the hair grower truly and honestly is, that is, "trusty," "honest," "genuine."

All that is asked is that you give Tatcho a chance to lay the foundation to a growth of natural thick and luxuriant hair. Give Tatcho this chance—let it prove to you that it lives up to its worthy name—Tatcho, the trusty, honest hair grower.

Ask your Chemist.

THE HAIR GROWER.

Tatcho

"Trusty," "Honest," "Genuine."